THRIVE

Thrive

Mindsets & Skillsets needed to succeed in a world dominated by smart machines & intelligent algorithms

Mukesh Gupta
Bangalore 2018

Copyright © 2018 by Mukesh Gupta
All rights reserved

For information about permission to reproduce selections from this book, write to mgr@rmukeshgupta.com

or

To,
Permissions,
Mukesh Gupta, 34, Sundar Murthy Road,
Cox Town, Bangalore 560005,
Karnataka, India
www.rmukeshgupta.com

For my son - Yuvan and all his friends!

This book is dedicated to my son and all the teenagers in the world who are growing up in a world that is slowly but definitely is being inhabited by as many smart machines and intelligent algorithms as many smart and intelligent people. I am hoping that they will find this book to be useful to learn from and thrive in the world that they are inheriting!

For all my friends and colleagues!

This book is also dedicated to all my friends and colleagues who are in the middle of their career and are facing the daunting task of re-inventing themselves and their careers as they go along. I know that it feels like changing tyres of a moving car. However, I also know that this reinvention is not only possible but even desirable, for it opens up a plethora of opportunities to be explored and exploited!

Table of Contents

AUTHOR'S NOTE 8

MINDSETS FOR THE DIGITAL AGE 11
- THE YA MINDSET 22
- THE DESIGNER'S MINDSET 29
- THE ENTREPRENEUR'S MINDSET 36
- THE SCIENTIFIC MINDSET 56
- THE TODDLER'S MINDSET 61
- THE PHILOSOPHER'S MINDSET 66
- THE ATHLETE'S MINDSET 70
- THE ACTOR'S MINDSET: 77
- HOW TO USE THE DIFFERENT MINDSETS: 83
- MINDSETS AS HABITS: 87

SKILLSETS 90
- LEARNING TO LEARN 92
- STAYING ANTI-FRAGILE 99
- BEING DATA SMART 111
- BEING EMOTIONALLY INTELLIGENT 118
- DEALING WITH ARTIFICIAL INTELLIGENCE 126
- BEING PERSUASIVE 134
- BEING CREATIVE 143
- AVOIDING ATTENTION TRAPS 152
- BEING CURIOUS 159
- BUILDING HABITS 163
- STORYTELLING: 168

IN CONCLUSION: 173

ABOUT THE AUTHOR: 174

ACKNOWLEDGEMENTS: 175

FURTHER RESOURCES: 176

Author's Note

There is not a single day that goes by when I don't hear someone talk about the pace of change around us and how businesses need to find their own version of digital transformation. There is also a lot of talk about what the future of work is going to look like.

There is also a lot of talk about machine learning and how robots and Artificial Intelligence (AI) are going to take over most of the regular jobs and that the displacement of work-force is going be of a magnitude that we have never seen before.

Artificial intelligence is already being deployed in place of lawyers to analyze court rulings and come up with plausible defense strategies that have the best probability of success. Artificial intelligence is also being deployed in the medical diagnosis field to analyze data from medical tests and detect diseases and there are a hundred other use cases that are being explored by technology startups and tech giants alike.

Startups working on AI and machine learning projects are getting funding at unprecedented levels. AI and machine learning capabilities are now becoming available as API's (small programs that allow anyone to use this capability inside of their own programs, as and when needed) that any startup in a garage can use to build new use cases for these technologies that will have the impact of taking away jobs from hundreds, if not hundreds of thousands of people losing their jobs to AI and machines.

Robots are taking the low-level automated jobs on the shop floor and AI powered software is taking away jobs from the higher end of jobs like software programmers, doctors, lawyers, journalists and business analysts.

Given that this is the world that we are expecting to move towards, we as a race need to think about how we as a race can respond to these changes.

At the same time, we find a trend where more and more people are finding themselves out of jobs and by necessity and at times by choice are working in project mode as consultants rather than employees. It is one thing to be an employee and a totally different thing to be on our own and work as consultants and on a project to project basis.

In this book, I try to answer the following question in detail:

> What can we do to "Thrive" in an increasingly digital world?

The answer I believe lies at the heart of the most human capability that exists – our mindsets and belief systems. Once we can develop the right mindsets and the accompanying belief systems, we can then identify and learn the skillsets that are required using the tools that are available to us.

This book is an attempt to identify the right mindsets, the accompanying belief system, the skillsets and the tools that we can use to learn the skillsets.

The book is divided into two parts:

- Mindsets – developing the mindset to thrive
- Skillsets – Identifying and developing the skills

I would recommend that you read the book in sequence. However, you can also directly launch into any of the parts and you will find that there is information that is available to you that can be put to use immediately to enable you to thrive.

By picking up this book, you have already taken the first step in your journey to not just stay relevant but to Thrive in the digital world.

Mukesh Gupta
April 2018

Mindsets for the Digital Age

Mindsets are the collection of our belief system that together informs and impacts all our action and reactions. Mindsets also determine how we behave in various situations. There are many definitions of mindsets. One that I think that is both simple to explain and understand is the following:

> *Mindsets are the operating system for our behavior. They create the confines of what we can and will most likely do.*

Our mind is a pattern matching machine. It is scientifically proven that a very small percentage of information that all our senses gather is processed by our brains. Based on this small percentage of information, our brain looks at the past patterns and fills in the blanks with our perceptions and known pathways to complete the picture. This is the reason why different people witnessing the exact same event can have a completely different recollection of the event.

Research has shown that we have two important parts of the brain that help us make sense of all the information that our sense organs capture. Without going into too much detail about our brain physiology, it is important that we understand how our brains function.

Assume that we decide to go on a vacation and book a flight out of our city to go to an exotic location, let's say Hawaii. Now, for us to reach there, we need to first reach the airport. Once we are there, we are first screened to ensure that we are not a potential threat to anyone who is flying. Our bags are screened and so are we. Once this is done, we are then directed to the various terminals and gates, relevant to the destination and the airline that we are travelling with. There they check if we are indeed booked to fly on that route and then we get to board the flight and fly away.

For our purposes, we can safely assume that our brain works roughly the same way that this airport functions.

The Threat detector:

The first filter is the threat detector. All the tourists that are arriving at the airport are like the various sensory inputs that our brains receive. The first thing that the brain does is to screen for any threats (perceived or real). Only when the brain doesn't detect any threat that it allows the input to proceed. This part of the brain that does threat detection is the oldest part of our brain and is hardwired to look out and help us survive.

This is also the part of the brain that is responsible for our primal emotions (love, fear, anger, ecstasy, trust and similar). This is also the part of the brain that is responsible for the fight or flight response (physiological and psychological) that we exhibit in our day-to-day life. Just in case the threat detection picks up something (perceived or real), then a different routine plays out. Just like the security protocols take over in an airport once there is a threat detected, the primal part of our brain takes control over our physiology, shuts down all non-critical functions, gets our hearts to pound, pumps adrenalin inside our body and creates a razor-sharp focus on the very thing that has threatened us. The body is now ready either to fight or flee.

The Gates of passage:

Once the brain doesn't perceive any threat, it allows information to flow to the right part of our brain where we think slower and rationally process information so that it can be acted upon appropriately. This is like the different passengers then going to the respective terminals and gates to take their respective flights out of the airport.

Mindsets:

Our mindsets are like the terminals or gates that we need to pass through to board the flight that will take us to our destinations. There are many of them. Just like you could only pass through one of them at a time, we have within us different mindsets that are active at different points in time, dependent on the time, situation and the environment that we are in.

The only difference is that we are constantly entering new airports instead of taking off in flights to our destinations. We move from one situation to another and the entire process takes place again and again. The only difference is that the gates that we pass through could be different every time. For most of us, the mindsets are so deeply ingrained that we don't even realize their presence within us. This is how we tend to react in any given situation. It's instinctive and super-fast.

The mindsets that we bring to a situation also depend on the situation itself. When we are a parent working with a child, we bring a different mindset. When we are in the office and talking to our superior, we bring a different mindset. When we are in the office and talking to someone who reports to us, we are in a different mindset. When we are happy and out on vacation, we bring in a different mindset.

While most of this is automatic, we do have control over what mindset we want to bring to play, if we want to.

It takes active work on ourselves and practice. This opportunity to control and decide which mindset we want to adopt in any given situation is what differentiates the wise men from all others. They are able to pick the right mindset for the right situation. This is a skill that we can all develop with the right practice. But in order to be able to do so, we need to have a reservoir of mindsets that we can pick out of. We can develop this reservoir of mindsets with practice.

In this book, we will cover some of the mindsets that can enable us to not only respond to the future that we envisage but to thrive in that future. We will try and understand the core beliefs of the different mindsets and also come up with a way to practice these mindsets in non-critical situations so that we can build the neural pathways needed to make these mindsets available to us in critical real-life scenarios.

I would like to share with you one example of how a mindset and the corresponding belief systems can affect our behavior.

In my case, early in my life (about 25 years ago), I was told by my cricket coach that while I had a good understanding of the game, I did not have the body type to compliment this understanding. This meant that if I nurtured any intention of playing the sport at a competitive level, I should drop it right then. When I asked for more information he shared with me that my ability to run quickly between wickets and the ability to field in positions other than close in was severely hampered as I was unable to run with any decent speed.

To top it all, I was made fun of, every time that I ended up on the field or running between the wickets. In addition, when I went for a routine physical examination to a doctor, he informed me that one of the bones in my nose actually extended and blocked one of my nostrils. This was a common problem and one that can be corrected any time by a routine surgery.

But by that time, I had a created a mindset for myself that I can be a good coach if I wanted to but can never be able to make a career out of playing the sport. This also meant that I had instilled a belief inside of me that I can't run fast as one of my nostrils is blocked, which leads me to huff and puff, even after a very small run. Not only this, I also started believing that I would not be able to do anything that requires me to control my breathing in any shape or form. This meant that I did not even try to learn to swim or to practice yoga.

Now, this belief has taken root so strongly that even after so many years and even knowing that this is not a rational belief, I have a mindset that ensures that either I don't end up in situations that require me to run. In case I can't avoid it, I try and inform everyone about my difficulty in running beforehand so that they don't make fun of me.

Is it true that I can't run fast because of the blocking of my nostril? Maybe, maybe not. But it is true to my mind and it ensures that I don't contradict this belief. So, I don't practice running, I don't get into situations that require me to run and I tell everyone around me that I can't run. Every single time that I talk about this, I end up reinforcing this belief and the strengthening the corresponding mindset.

Now, is it possible for me to overcome this mindset and learn how to run, swim or be able to do all the breathing yogic exercises? I sure think it is possible. Have I been able to change this mindset yet? As I write this I am in the process of working on this belief. By the time I finish writing this book, I am hoping to have a different mindset and have overcome this debilitating belief system.

What follows in this book is the process which I am using to bring about this transformation within myself.

Mindsets by Carol Dweck:

The thinking and conversation around mindsets was brought about in public consciousness by the path-breaking work of Carol Dweck that she summarized in her best-selling book "Mindsets".

In her book, she shares her experience of working with kids.

She was running an experiment with kindergarten kids by giving them puzzles to solve. As part of this experiment she observed that when some kids got a puzzle which they could not solve, they would want to continue to work on it and enjoyed the challenge. Then there were some other kids who when got stuck with a puzzle, quickly lost interest in the puzzle and went back to puzzles they knew how to solve. This was intriguing enough for Carol to run a much more detailed research project that ran for years and that resulted in her best-selling book.

To summarize, she found that what differentiated the kids was their mindset towards solving the challenging puzzle.

1. Growth Mindset
2. Fixed Mindset

Let's try and understand what each of these mindsets mean for us. It is absolutely critical for our progress as this is the meta understanding based on which we can learn all other mindsets and continue to evolve and grow.

Growth Mindset:

We have a growth mindset if

- We believe that we can continue to learn and evolve our intelligence.
- We believe that we can learn new skills, change our beliefs and opinions when new information surfaces.
- We believe that we are in control of ourselves and our behaviors and it is possible to change our behaviors and how we react to certain stimuli.
- We believe that there is no age limit to learn new skills.
- We believe that we can learn to respond to stimuli, rather than react to it, then we have a growth mindset.

In order for us to effect a change in our behavior, it is not enough to just look at the behavior in isolation but to also look at the mindset and the set of beliefs that are causing us to behave in that specific manner. Lasting change is only possible if we not only address the specific behavior but also the underlying mindset.

This mindset is characterized by the following motto:

> *"I don't know, yet. Let's find out!"*

Fixed Mindset:

We have a fixed mindset if

- We believe that we are fully formed, and that adult behavior change is a myth.
- We believe that talent is innate and there is nothing much that we can do about it. You either have it or you don't.
- We think that no amount of effort and practice can make you good at something for which you don't have the talent for.

When we are in a fixed mindset, we tend to behave as if our cups are full and that there is no space to learn anything new. When we are in this mindset, we tend to stick to known pastures and not venture out. This is the mindset which creates and maintain "status quo".

This mindset is characterized by this motto:

> *We are either good at something or we are not!*

As you can see, we can continue to grow and evolve if we have the growth mindset. This is the first mindset that we need to adopt if we are to understand all the other mindsets that we will talk about going ahead in the book.

What follows next is the different mindsets and the associated belief systems that make up the mindset. There is a certain process that we need to follow to be able to internalize the belief system.

We first need to believe that we can learn new mindsets. This is already true for all of us. For example, nobody teaches us to adopt the mindset of a parent when our first child arrives. We already have inside of us everything that we need in order to learn new mindsets, the accompanying belief systems and make it available for us to pick and choose from, when needed.

Secondly, we need to be able to find low stake situations and practice the mindsets, the belief's and the accompanying behaviors. We will talk about it with examples, as and when we discuss each of the mindsets.

Lastly, it is important to continue to practice these behaviors to a level where it becomes second nature for us. We will learn about a specific way to practice called deliberate practice, which enables us to continue to grow at a fast pace.

Let's look at the different mindsets that can and will play an integral and important part in our lives if we are to thrive in an increasingly digital world, with more and more work being done by machines and rampant use of artificial intelligence all around us.

The YA Mindset

Apart from the growth and fixed mindset, I strongly believe that there are many other mindsets that can help influence our behaviors and play a significant role in our growth. One of them is the mindset of improv artists.

The first such mindset comes to us from the world of improvisational comedy. This is the form of live performance where a set of actors are given a situation and they have to respond to the situation, without any prompts or pre-defined script. This form of theatre requires for the actors to be completely present and improvise on each others performance as there is no script and they haven't practiced any of these situations before.

The first and most important rule in improv comedy is that you need to accept whatever your partner has put in play. You always use the "Yes... And ..." mindset to move the plot ahead. The moment you disagree with what your partner has put in place, the plot gets stuck and it gets a lot more difficult to get out of that situation.

It is very similar in our real lives as well. Our partner in this case is life itself. Whatever life throws at us, if we use the "Yes And" mindset, we are not only accepting what life has given to us but are also adding our own bit to it. This is a great attitude to have to deal with any challenge that life can throw at us. This is also a great mindset to be in when we are trying to create something from nothing.

This is also a great mindset to be in when we are trying to be creative as a team. We build on each other's ideas and we will find that we have the potential to be much more creative as a team than we could ever be as individuals.

This mindset also allows us to take risk. This also demands that we be completely present in the current moment.

Rules of Improv and hence the YA Mindset is as below:

<u>Rule no. 1: Agree.</u>

You have to first agree to what has come before you. In real life, this means that you have to agree and accept whatever you have been handed or the situation that you find yourself in. It is also about not wanting anything else than what you have already been given. In life, in any moment, we are given a set of options, circumstances, tools, information and situations. These are the raw materials for us. In order to work with them, we must first come to agree or accept that these are the ingredients that we will need to work with. There is nothing more and nothing less.

Rule No.2: Yes And...

Once we have accepted our current reality, we need to internalize it and use the material at our disposal to think about what is possible with this material. We use our imagination and add something to this mixture of raw materials at our disposal. We combine, connect and imagine stuff to move towards a potentially good place. Irrespective of where we find ourselves, we always possess the ability and the audacity to move towards a place that is good for us.

Rule No.3: Make statements.

Improv artists are always trained to make statements rather than ask questions of their partner. They are always trained to be part of the solution. The same is true with our lives. Instead of posing questions to others, complaining about stuff, it is much better to make statements, use the power of our imagination and come up with ideas that make our lives better. This way we are always in control of our destinations.

Rule No.4: There are no mistakes.

In improv, there are no mistakes. Irrespective of what we say or do, our partners need to accept that as truth, agree with it and build upon it. The same is true in our lives. There are no mistakes. We just need to accept where we are and what we have and use this reality as raw material to cook up where we want to go.

As they say, we are only in control of our reaction to things that happen around us. The moment we give up the illusion of control on everything other than our actions and reactions, we feel free of frustrations and anger. Once we are able to deal with these, we are then able to accept that which is given to us as raw material and get to work.

There have been many instances in my life (as I am sure in your life as well) when something that I thought was a mistake, ended up either leading me to a great opportunity or helped me learn an important lesson that helped me in a difficult situation later on. Remember, there are no mistakes.

<u>Rules No.5: Place all of your attention on your partner.</u>

In improv, if you are not present in the moment and fully focused on your partner and his or her take on the situation, it is extremely difficult for you to build on their takes. The same is true in our lives. If we are present in the moment, we can look at all that comes our way and see how we can use them in our journey.

Rule No.6: Leave no one behind.

This is in reference to the team spirit in which improv is done. Every act of improv is first and foremost a team act. As in any good team, no one is left behind. Team mates take care of each other and help each other. When someone is stuck, they help them get unstuck. They strive to give each other opportunities to shine. The same is true in our lives as well. The more we realize that irrespective of what we do in our life, it takes a team to do it. The motto of any good team is to not leave any one on the team behind.

Cultivating this mindset is not easy. It takes a great deal of practice and hard work. But once mastered, this mindset can have a huge impact on our lives and how we lead our lives. This mindset also gives us a unique perspective to leading our lives.

This mindset is characterized by the motto:

Yes, And, there are no mistakes in life!

Putting this in practice:

This is probably the easiest to put in practice. All we need to do is to pick about 15-20 minutes a day or at least about 30 minutes in a week and set it aside to practicing the YA mindset. You bring in your friends, spouses or children along and play some of the improv games.

Some improv games that you could play are the following:

<u>Stuck in a Situation with You (SiSY):</u>

In this game, pick out one of your favorite scenes from a movie and pick a character that you will play and another character that your partner will play. You start the scene and let the partner react to it. You need to play out the scene not as it plays out in the movie but in your own private way based on your own imagination.

The idea is to continue to play out the scene for at least 5 minutes without breaking the rules mentioned above. This may seem simple but believe me it is not simple. But with practice, you can learn to play the game without breaking the rules for up to about 10 minutes. You then switch the roles and enact the scene again.

<u>Words Added Randomly to Speech (WARS):</u>

In this game, you pick out 15-20 words randomly from a dictionary and write each one in a separate piece of paper. Fold them and shuffle them. Each one picks one of the pieces and you speak on a topic extempore. You can decide the topic yourself or you can also select one randomly.

Once you start talking about the topic, at the end of every minute, you are handed one of the words that were picked randomly, and you are to incorporate that word in your speech. You continue this way for about 5 minutes with each person getting at least 5 random words to be incorporated in their speech.

These are simple exercises that can be used as a form of play and by doing so, we are creating practice in low stake situations, so that we are able to internalize the rules and belief systems for this mindset. Once we are able to do this, this mindset is then available for us to use when we call for it.

The Designer's Mindset

Every profession has a certain method that they use to go about their business. Designers usually think and behave differently than people from any other professions.

For good designers

- The utility of the object that they are designing is important.
- So are the aesthetics of their design.

They believe in the power of "And" and not in "Or". They don't think in terms of beauty or functionality. They think about designing beauty and functionality.

Some belief's that are central to this mindset are:

- There is no single right answer. There is my approach and then there is your approach. There are always a lot of options to address a challenge or a problem. We only need to explore them and pick something that works for us.
- Constraints (Real or self-inflicted) play a critical role in their craft.
- Individuality is really important in this mindset. Each designer brings forth his own unique style

and individuality to everything that he or she designs.
- Prototyping and testing is an integral part of problem solving.
- Simplest design that allows the right usage of the design is the best design.

When presented with a problem to be solved or a challenge to be addressed, good designers always use the framework outlined below.

<u>Look:</u>

The first thing that a designer does when presented with a design challenge is to look at the challenge through different lenses. Looking is a skill that can be learnt by all of us. Most of us see but don't look. One is a passive act and the other is an active act. When we look, we observe, internalize and are looking at something with an active interest in it. We will talk about looking in much more detail later in the book. This is a skill that each one of us must learn if we are to thrive in a world where our ability to be creative is going to be of paramount importance.

<u>Think:</u>

Once the designer looks at the different aspects of the design challenge, they then take some time and internalize all that they have seen. They think about the different patterns that they see or rather not see. They think about what aspect of the challenge needs further investigation and why. What should be the objectives of this further observations. At the end of this phase, good designers are able to create hypothesis about the challenges based on their understanding of the underlying system.

Do:

Based on this hypothesis, they then look at either confirming their hypothesis or to negate it. In order to do so, they create experiments and try potential solutions for the challenge that they are trying to address. They are unrestrained when it comes to the ideas for their experiments. Once they have a bunch of creative ideas, they will then pick a few of the ideas where they see the most potential and test them out by creating low fidelity prototypes, which are easy and quick to put together.

Learn:

The reason for them to test these ideas is to learn if these ideas are solving the challenge. If yes, how and if not, why not. This helps them test their hypothesis. The primary purpose of doing this is also to learn if any of the assumptions that the designers had while brainstorming are real or are imaginary. They are also able to learn from the testing what part of the challenge is more important than others. They also learn what works and what doesn't, which then guides them through to the next iteration.

Repeat:

Once they have their learnings, the designers start the process all over again. They will look at the learnings from different perspectives, pick one that they would like to test further, develop the prototype, test it so they can learn more about the challenge and their potential solutions. This process continues until they are satisfied with their solution.

Diverge and Converge:

If we look at the framework closely, we will find that at every stage of the process, designers follow the diverge and converge process. They will always create more options and follow it by picking out an option from the bunch, test it out, learn from it and repeat the process. This divergence and convergence is the most fundamental action that a designer does to solve their design challenge. They continue to do that until they find a solution that solves the design challenge to their satisfaction.

The belief system that makes up the designer's mindset can be a great asset to have in our lives, irrespective of whether we are designers or not.

Designers share the belief that there is never "<u>A Right Answer</u>" but there are "<u>multitudes of potential right answers</u>" to almost all our problems. This fundamental belief can enable us not to get stuck to find that right answer and feel defeated if we don't find that right answer. This enables us to quickly recover from any roadblocks that we encounter in our journey and look at the other options. There are always other options.

Designers believe that Constraints are important to the creative process. In life, if there is one thing that is certain, it is constraints. We would be much more relaxed and at peace if we start to believe that constraints are an integral part of our struggle to solve any of life's challenge and that we should welcome it, maybe even create some artificial constraints, rather than feel bogged down by them.

The belief that we can prototype an idea or a solution quickly and test it out is critical when we are trying to overcome seemingly unsurmountable challenges. This is the way out. This helps us not to feel overwhelmed by the challenge as we can ideate, prototype and test rapidly, thereby increasing our knowledge about what is working and what is not. This enables us to scale any kind of challenge that can be thrown at us.

This mindset is characterized by the motto:

There is never a single Right Answer!

Putting this in practice:

I play this very interesting game. My job requires me to travel quite a bit. When you travel a lot, you end up visiting a lot of new places – hotels, airports, customer locations and the whole bit.

What I do when I go to a new place is be observant of the way things are designed around there.

Sometimes I find that it is not so intuitive to figure out how to use a tap in a rest room.

One other time I found that there was a notice on top of a washroom flush requesting people to just push and not turn the flush button.

Then one time I found that one side of a two-door entrance would open when pushed and the other side would open when pulled. I constantly saw people struggle with the door, pulling the side that needed to be pushed and pushing the side that needed to be pulled.

Another time, I saw that the way cars were directed to the parking lot in a mall was confusing. Almost all the drivers had a tough time figuring out how to exit.

In every one of these situations, I would stop for a minute and think about what other options were available for the designers of these products or services. Why did they pick these instead of the others? What would I have done if I were the one who had to design this? Why?

It takes but a couple of minutes in the moment to notice and register the situation. And you could think about the questions I have just listed above when you have sometime (in my case, when I was on a flight or when I was watching TV or even at times when I was about to go to bed), basically, whenever you have a few moments to yourself.

This entire process of thinking through the design of everyday things helps you develop the designer's mindset and again in very low stakes environments. Once you have enough practice, this mindset then becomes available for you to access as and when you need to.

The Entrepreneur's Mindset

We are moving towards a world where most of us will be either entrepreneurs or solopreneurs (one person business, typically a consultant working for themselves). The time when you completed a good college education, entered the workforce as an employee and rose in the corporate ladder (either within the same organization or in some other organization) to become a senior vice-president or if you are good and lucky end-up as a CEO is going to vanish sooner than we may think.

Today, we have machines which can work as assembly line workers, hotel clerks, concierge, nurses, companions for elders, lawyers, doctors, drivers, artists, journalists, gamers, coaches, board members and many more.

The value proposition for businesses to employ more and more machines is strong and will get stronger with the increasing capabilities and complexities of these machines and dropping costs.

Add to this, the already accelerating trend of organizations looking to hire contract employees rather than full-time employees, both to reduce cost and to leverage the global talent pool rather than limit themselves to the local talent pool.

This means, that we, as a race will be forced to look at opportunities beyond these traditional jobs. We would need to either be the kind of people who know how to create these machines or know how to work with these machines or be able to add value where these machines can't already add value.

When we look at all of these put together, whether we like it or not, there is a good chance that we might end up either as an entrepreneur, a solopreneur or a contract employee.

We are fast moving to becoming a society of entrepreneurs rather than a society dominated by employees. This will have an impact on every aspect of society – from how we educate our children to how we govern our citizens and everything in between.

An entrepreneur is someone who sees every challenge, complaint or issue as a potential opportunity to be solved. He/she then picks up one that is close to him or where (s)he sees the biggest opportunity and goes about to address that challenge.

Some of the most important belief's that good entrepreneurs operate on are as below:

1. There is a seed of opportunity in every situation.
2. They are comfortable in making decisions.

3. They have a bias towards action.
4. They are comfortable with ambiguity.
5. They believe that there is no failure or success that is permanent.
6. They bring in an outsider's perspective
7. They beget change.
8. They find & mitigate risks.
9. They are able to move people.

Seed of Opportunity:

Good entrepreneurs always find a seed of opportunity in everything that they encounter or experience.

When Richard Branson was mistreated by British Airways, he went on to start Virgin Airlines.

When Elon Musk was frustrated by traffic jams enroute to work, he created a new business - "The Boring Company".

When Ratan Tata saw a couple getting drenched in a motor cycle during monsoon rain, he decided to build an affordable car that doesn't cost much more than the motorcycle itself.

These are just examples of some of the most successful entrepreneurs finding opportunity where everyone else finds fault and complains.

There are countless examples of such behaviors by entrepreneurs where they find opportunity that is hiding in plain sight which all of us miss. In hindsight, they look at the same thing that all of us see everyday and yet are able to find the opportunity amidst the chaos that we see. This is primarily because we are not looking for it.

Have you ever noticed that once you decide to buy a specific model of car, all of a sudden you start seeing a lot of them all around you? It is not as if suddenly there are a lot of cars of that model on the street. They were always there, we just didn't notice them. Once we decide to buy the car, our subconscious mind gives importance to this model of the car and brings it to our conscious attention every time it sees it, while masking something else from our conscious attention. This is the reason why sometime after we actually buy the car, we stop seeing them all around us.

It's exactly the same phenomenon that is at work here with entrepreneurs. Once you start looking for opportunities everywhere you go, in every situation that you encounter, your subconscious mind realizes that this is what is important to you and then will actually help you find opportunities that are hidden in plain sight. It is all a matter of practice and intent.

Putting this in practice:

This is not so easy to put in practice. So, I will borrow a concept from BJ Fogg and his "Tiny Habits" philosophy. He has created this Tiny Habits course together that anyone of us can join. In this practical, almost automated course he teaches us how we can build tiny habits by practicing something daily for about 30 days. He also lays down a formula that helps us.

He first asks us to identify the habit that we want to build. In this case, we want to be able to see opportunity that is present all around us.

He then says that we need to create an anchor for the habit. For example, I will do "this" after/before/while doing "that". We can use the same formula to build a habit of finding opportunities every day. The easiest way to finding opportunities is looking for them disguised as complaints.

So, one way to look at combining both these insights can come up with the following formula.

- I will look for an opportunity every time I complain or hear someone complain about anything.

So, for example, you find yourself complaining about the traffic. You will then think about what opportunity does traffic provide us. In this case, it provides us captive audience, which radio capitalizes by selling that attention to people who want this attendance (advertisers).

So, what else can be done with this attention? As Zig Ziglar used to say, we can convert this ride as a university where people can learn.

- You could create a service which picks a random topic and breaks it down so you can learn about it in an hour or half or even 15 mins.
- You could create a service where you rent-a-chauffeur anywhere in the city on-demand, who can drive you wherever you want to, so you can use that time to do something productive, maybe work, talk to friends or relatives or even answer some emails (though it may or may not be productive based on how you use your emails).
- You could also provide a taxi service, which comes with its own salon or massage or any such thing. This way your customers can not just travel from one place to another in your taxies but also feel more beautiful along the way.

These are just a few examples that I have thought of. It does require some practice but once you start this practice, you will be surprised at the sheer number of opportunities that are staring right at us.

Decisiveness:

Good entrepreneurs are comfortable making decisions. They look at all the options that are available to them. They look at the opportunities that are available and are comfortable making their choices. They know that not all of their decisions will turn out to be right. They intuitively know that if you don't decide and act, you don't have a shot at anything worthwhile.

Good entrepreneurs also have a clear manifesto (stated or otherwise) which guides them in their decision making. For example, one entrepreneur that I know well is Kumar (name changed). He has a set of rules for people related decisions, process related decisions, resources related decisions. He uses these rules to make his decisions and move ahead. These rules can also be called heuristics. This is how we make decisions intrinsically as well. We have certain heuristics already in our brains whether we know about them or not.

Kumar knows that not all of these decisions that he makes may turn out to be good decisions. However, he knows that most of them would be good (some even great in hindsight), some of them could have been better had he waited for more information before he made the decision and some could potentially be bad decisions. What he does is that whenever one of the decisions turn out to be a bad one, he reflects on the decision and the rule that he had used to make it. He then thinks and decides if there is a change in that rule needed. If yes, he adjusts that rule, else, just moves on.

Putting in practice:

Just like Kumar has his heuristics, we all can build our very own rules to making decisions as well. If not in every aspect of our lives, we need to create these rules in at least those aspects of life, which we hold important for us.

In my case, I was diagnosed as a diabetic a couple of years back and my doctors indicated that I need to get in shape (lose about 15 kgs) and get on medication. I love listening to interesting podcasts and hated going to the gym. So, I made a rule for myself – I will listen to podcasts only when I go for a walk.

I have difficulty deciding on stuff to buy for home. This drives my wife crazy as we would go shopping for a piece of furniture, explore everything that is available in the market, decide on a particular piece and I will develop cold feet. The entire process would start again and end the same way again.

As I write this we are in the process of buying furniture again and this time, I have decided the following rule – if my wife likes the furniture, I buy the furniture. I don't want to think about whether I like it, whether it is priced right or any other thing. I defer the analysis of all aspect of the furniture to my wife and go with her judgement.

This doesn't mean that I don't participate in the decision. I will share my opinion about the furniture but will buy it if my wife likes it, irrespective of my opinion. This may or may not be the best way to make a decision, but it is a rule that I will go with and adjust if this leads to bad decisions.

Another area in my life where I find it difficult to make decisions is when it is time to have difficult conversations. I seem to procrastinate on this and delay have the conversation. So, I created the rule that I will not defer a difficult conversation for more than 24 hours. Once I know that I need to have a difficult conversation, I will have it within 24 hours of that realization, irrespective of how difficult the conversation might be.

I have also created a personal manifesto by which I want to lead my life. It is available publicly on my blog. These are the rules by which I want to make decisions and live my life. This way, I am intentional about my decisions and at the same time able to decide and move ahead.

You can also create a set of rules that will help you make decisions in your life

Bias for action:

What differentiates people who have a lot of ideas and true entrepreneurs is that entrepreneurs take action on the ideas that they feel have the potential. If you are an aspiring entrepreneur, this is the single most important thing that you could incorporate to take the plunge and become an entrepreneur. Even if you don't want to become an entrepreneur, it is important to develop this bias for action in our lives. Action creates a feedback loop that can enable us to learn and move ahead in our lives.

As the old proverb goes – "Water is pure only as long as it moves". Most things that get stagnant get worse. This includes people as well. We need to continue to move and that movement comes with action.

Putting in Practice:

In the above example about finding opportunity in being stuck in traffic, here is what I did.

I decided that I want to use this time effectively for learning. So, I subscribed to Audible.com and a host of podcasts (on varying topics). This has enabled me to have at least 30 audiobooks and about 30-40 podcast episodes that I could listen to on my phone at any point in time.

When I ride my car to office or back home, I put on one of these on the car and listen to them. This has enabled me to learn so much from such a wide variety of people. This is something that would have never been possible, had I just continued to complain.

This is exactly what I mean by a bias for action. I am sure many of my friends want to do something similar, but it is not enough to want something.

It is the next step that is both simple yet difficult to execute – which is to actually go ahead and take action that will move you forward with your decision. You need to subscribe to audible or similar service. Pick a few books and download them on your phone. Then you need to remember to play them while you are driving and listen to them. All of these can happen only if you have a bias to take action.

Friends with Ambiguity:

Good entrepreneurs realize that there will always be a certain amount of ambiguity around us. We can never be certain about everything. Someone wise once said, that something will always go wrong. We can always count on that. What will go wrong might be difficult to predict, but it's easy to predict that something will go wrong. Once we know this, we can incorporate this in our planning so that we are not taken by surprise at a later date.

Entrepreneurs offer a hand of friendship towards ambiguity. They learn to live with it. They never crave for full certainty. This enables them to decide quickly and continue to develop their bias for action. We will delve deeper into this particular skill when we explore skillsets needed to Thrive.

The Impermanent nature of success and failure:

Good entrepreneurs know that neither success nor failure is permanent. They intuitively understand this and act accordingly. They know that by experience – they have seen and experienced success from the brink of failure and vice versa. They know that as entrepreneurs there is only one way to think and act – to continue to work towards a worthy goal and grow. They understand that the only thing that is permanent is the wheel of change.

They also have uncommon belief in their ability to be creative enough to find the seeds of success from every failure and that every success has the seeds of failure within it, which if not addressed correctly, has the potential to kill all the success.

Putting in practice:

As we have learnt earlier, we tend to find what we are actively and sub-consciously looking for. We need to believe that every moment in our life has the seeds for both success and failure, in whatever way we define them.

We can make a habit out of this by practicing it in low stake situations, in not just our lives but in the lives of everyone around us (friends, family or public figures). We live in times when there is a deluge of negativity all around us. All you need to do is to switch on the NEWS or open a newspaper, and we will find all the adversity that we need.

All we need to do is the following:

- When we come across someone we know personally who is going through a tough time, can we think of at least 3 things in his or her current situation that has the potential for their future success or well-being?

- When we come across someone we know personally who is celebrating his or her success and come up with at least 3 things that in his or her current situation that has the potential for destroying the very success that they are celebrating?
- Can we look at the newspaper every Saturday and do these very exercises (seeds of success or failure) for people whom we don't know personally but are being presented in the paper?

Once we have done this a dozen times, we can then look at exploring answers to the same set of questions for ourselves and in our current situation. This helps keep us on our toes.

Outsider's perspective:

Good entrepreneurs usually bring an outsider's perspective to any problem that they are trying to address through their enterprise. It is this outsider's perspective that gives them the edge over the incumbents. They identify and bring in new ways to solve old problems. They are able to defy conventional wisdom by using contemporary wisdom. They realize that over time, there are new technologies that become available, new processes become standardized, new thinking becomes pervasive and when you combine these together with other qualities that good entrepreneurs possess, we have a potent recipe for disruption.

As good entrepreneurs understand that there are many ways to solve any particular problem, they are not afraid to look at the problem from different perspectives. They use their imagination to look at the problem they are trying to solve and see if any of the new technologies, processes or thinking can help them solve the problem differently, they also look at the existing ways of solving a problem and are not satisfied with that. They are driven to find out if they can themselves solve the problem better, faster or cheaper. This drive is what keeps them on the lookout for potential perspectives to solve the problem.

Putting in Practice:

One creative exercise that I have used multiple times in my workshops and in my personal projects is the following:

I pick a specific problem that I would like to solve. Then I introduce an artificial constraint – say using a specific technology or at a specific cost or using a specific material. Once you have introduced this constraint, you are automatically forced to think from a different perspective. You then come up with ideas and solutions that conventional thinking would never throw up. This then gives the opportunity to think as an outsider and hence disrupt incumbents.

There are some constraints that could work in most situations. They are

1. How can you solve the problem at half the cost?
2. How can you solve the problem without using any of the component used by its current solution?
3. Is this really the problem? Is there a deeper more important problem to be solved?
4. What happens if you skip the problem? How can you skip the problem?
5. If you had access to any technology in the world, how would you solve this problem?

You can be as creative as you want to be to introduce the constraints. With experience, we can learn what kinds of constraints work with what kinds of problems and with that the kinds of solutions that we can think of can also get very creative and out-of-the-box.

Risk Mitigators:

It is a common perception that good entrepreneurs are risk takers. My experience tells me that they are not risk takers at all. As a matter of fact, they are risk mitigators. They obsess on finding the risks in their decisions and mitigate them before going ahead with their plans.

They will always find a way to minimize the risk that any of their steps entail. Good entrepreneurs usually ask themselves the question – "What is the worst that can happen if I take a specific course of action?" and follow it up with the question – "what can I do to ensure that it doesn't happen?".

They also use the following question to limit the size of risk that they are willing to take – "What is my risk tolerance on this project? How much money/time/fame/name or whatever can I risk on this project? When is it enough and time to pull the plug?". By knowing the maximum risk that they are willing to expose themselves to right at the start, they know when to stop investing or taking a specific course. They know when it is time to change course or accept failure. Either ways they will reflect on what happened and learn from it.

Putting in practice:

Building this belief is a matter of asking the same questions that good entrepreneurs ask themselves while evaluating risk on any given project.

1. How much risk can I take on this? How much is too much?
2. What is the worst that can happen if I take a specific approach?
3. What can I do to avoid that from happening?

Repeat these questions for 2 - 3 rounds and you would have mitigated the risk.

One very important thing for us to note here is that despite assessing the risk and mitigating it, good entrepreneurs always take action. The bias for action is more self-evident in this situation than in any other situation.

<u>They move people:</u>

Almost everything worth doing takes a team to do it well. Good entrepreneurs know and understand that. They possess the ability to move people and get them to see and buy into their vision, one way or other. They understand people and what makes people tick. They understand the psychology of people intuitively and use this understanding to use the right persuasive method with the right people.

As they say in India, they are adept at using Saam (logic), Daam (incentives), Dand (deterrents) and bhed (insinuation or emotional appeal) appropriately, as needed.

This makes them capable of building good teams and with the right motivations. Like all of us, entrepreneurs are also humans and can make mistakes in judging people and their motivations. What separates good entrepreneurs from all the others is that they recognize their mistakes and act quickly to correct the same. This quality shows up across all the other belief systems and is a character trait of good entrepreneurs.

Putting in practice:

This is probably the most difficult or the easiest skill to practice depending on our own tendencies when it comes to understanding people and what motivates them. While for most of us this comes naturally, some of us need to constantly learn and work on this as a skill.

For most of us, just using one of the four techniques don't work. We need to use a combination of these techniques. We need to observe the words that people use to understand their own pre-dispositions towards a particular kind of influence, so that we can use the same technique with them.

For example, if the person we are trying to enroll continues to use data or logic while speaking, that seems to be their preferred means of communication. We then need to use the same technique to communicate with them.

Similarly, if the person we are trying to enroll continues to use emotional words like, "I feel", "It seems", etc., we need to match that with the same technique and use emotional appeal to communicate with them and win them over.

So, the ability that we need to practice is listening. Pick a specific conversation with a specific person that we are scheduled for or any random one-on-one conversation and listen for these words. Try and identify if the person you are speaking to favors a specific kind of technique. Do this at least once a day with at least one conversation, so that we are able to build that muscle and capability.

If despite doing this, we find it tough to find out the technique preferred by the person, the easiest way for us to learn is to ask them – what motivates them? What moves them? Then see for ourselves if the answer we get aligns with their actions. IF it does, we know how to enroll and move them and if it doesn't then we go back and talk to them again, this time with based on our experience.

The Scientific Mindset

The scientific mindset is about following the scientific process to understand things around us. The scientific process gives equal importance to what we can and do observe around us and how this observation can be explained.

The scientific method is the following:

Observation:

Usually, all scientific enquiry starts with an observation. Why does a specific thing occur, or it doesn't occur? Does the sun go around the earth or does the earth go around the sun? Why does the apple fall down? Why and when does an eclipse occur? Why do we see the lightning first and the thunder follows? Why do we have long days in summer and longer nights in winter? Why do some people living in a small village in Japan have the highest average lifespan in the world and so forth?

Explanation or Hypothesis:

Then a scientist thinks about the observation and creates a hypothesis based on his or her understanding of what is happening. For example, the hypothesis for the reason that some people in an obscure village in Japan have the highest average lifespan is due to their lifestyle choices – what they eat (specific food) and how they spend their time (in a community, with friends, doing low intensity exercising, gardening, etc.).

Experimentation:

Once the hypothesis has been arrived at, the scientists then design an experiment to test the hypothesis. They will create a control group and an experimental group and run the experiment and closely record their observations. They check if the observations are in accordance with what the hypothesis predicted or not. If it is, they will continue to design a new experiment and follow the entire process again. IF the result is not what the hypothesis predicted, then they change the hypothesis and continue to run the experiments. The primary purpose of doing these experiments is to prove that the hypothesis is wrong. If they are unable to prove it wrong, that hypothesis then becomes a law or a principle and is widely accepted to be true by the scientific community.

Publish their results:

This is one of the most important reasons for our progress in the scientific field. All scientists are expected to publish their hypothesis and the results from their experiments in scientific journals, irrespective of the success of their experimentation.

This allows other scientists to build on top of what someone else has already done, without having to re-invent the wheel all over again.

Theory-in-practice:

When many scientists, through their various experiments continue to find that the hypothesis consistently is able to predict the results of the experiments, they then consider the hypothesis as the theory that explains the initial observation. But only until it is proven wrong. It is exactly this practice and mindset that has enabled the scientific community to continue to evolve our understanding of our environments and our bodies. This ability to look at the objective proof and accept that the older theory could be wrong is what enables scientific progress.

This is not to say that everything is smooth and working really well, but for the most part, our scientists have done well, apart from a few instances.

This mindset is characterized by the motto:

> *Hypothesis is True until proven otherwise*

Putting in practice:

This is a great mindset to be in, when we want to understand something that we currently don't understand. The scientific process gives a very precise, time tested process for us to figure things out. We subconsciously use this process all the time – when we join a new team or are in a new environment and want to understand and make up our mind about whom to trust and whom not to.

Again, this is a skill that we can all learn, starting with low stakes situations. Make an observation at work or at home. Then try to understand what could have caused the observation and make a hypothesis about it. Once you have the hypothesis, put it to test by either by designing an experiment or making further observation, but from a different perspective or at a different time.

Let's say, you have observed that the sales of a specific product in your product line has suddenly taken off and has been way above your expectation or way below your expectation. Based on your understanding of the situation, try to come up with a hypothesis that can explain the current trend. Once you have the same, then set up an experiment to test it. One hypothesis could be that your competition has run out of that specific product and so all the demand in the market is coming to you. IF that is the hypothesis, you can test it out by asking one of your customers or prospects if that is true. One other hypothesis could be that it is easier for your sales team to sell this product than the other products and so they are always positioning this product and not the other products from your suite. You can then design an experiment to test it (you go on a few sales calls to check if your hypothesis is true).

You may ask how is it different from what we already do? The difference is that we think of our assumption as a hypothesis that needs to be proven right or wrong, i.e., the hypothesis could be right or wrong (not us). This enables us to not blindly act on our first assumption or hypothesis. This also makes it easier for us to dump the first hypothesis if that turns out to be wrong as we don't identify it with us.

Not being able to change the first assumption that we come up with to explain our observation and getting stuck with it could very well be the single most important reason for billions of dollars in losses and hundreds and thousands of divorces in the world.

The Toddler's Mindset

Every time we find ourselves in a completely new environment and have the need to learn and make a fresh start, the best mindset to adopt is the toddler's mindset. A toddler is not worried about looking bad. A toddler doesn't complain about how tough it is to learn to walk or to talk. A toddler doesn't get bored trying to learn new stuff. A toddler's mindset is a beginner's or a learner's mindset.

The mindset is defined by curiosity, total lack of fear of failure, complete dedication to learning new skills and is one in which practice is of paramount importance. Everything that a toddler learns is through practice. Not just any kind of practice but a certain kind of practice – deliberate practice.

Let's try and understand how a toddler learns to talk. It is the same process by which the toddler learns all the other skills. So, how does a toddler learn to talk?

The toddler has a set of teachers (parents, siblings, etc.) who are going to teach the toddler to learn new skills. The toddler sees and hears what everyone around her is talking. She then tries to repeat what she hears. The parents break down the language into simple words to start with – mom or dad. They keep repeating the words to the toddler and encourage the toddler to repeat. When she tries to repeat and gets even remotely close to sounding like the word, everyone around her is excited and are laughing and hugging her. Asking even more people to come around and again ask her to repeat the word and doing the same thing. The toddler meanwhile understands that she is doing something right and constantly repeats the words. One day, she gets the sounds exactly right. Everyone is celebrating and hugs and kisses abound. The toddler is very happy as well.

But then suddenly the hugs and kisses are no longer available for repeating these words. The elders around are now trying to teach the toddler new words. The toddler understands that the only way to get the hugs and kisses and all the attention again is by getting the new sounds right. It continues to practice with the help of the elders around and finally gets these new words as well. This process continues and the toddler continues to learn.

What we can learn from this entire process is the following:

Teacher or Coach:

To learn something new, we need a teacher or a coach who believes that we have the capability to learn the stuff. The coach also needs to be able to understand our ability

- And help us decide the kind of practice we need to improve
- And provide critical feedback so we can learn faster and better.
- And correctly identify our mistakes and helps remove them.
- And provides us encouragement through the process.
- And celebrates our success with us.

This teacher or coach can be in person with us or could be virtual. If we can't find someone who could be with us and help us train, we could also enroll ourselves in an online training or even start learning from a book. Though not as effective as having a coach is, they are also a good way to learn.

Another way to learn from someone is to look for someone who is good at something that we want to learn and ask them to teach it to us either by allowing us to observe them exhibiting that behavior (shadowing) or by sharing their insights with us (explaining) or by doing both – first observing then explaining what we observe.

I have used this technique to have conversations with more than 60 people and learn from each one of them. I am talking about my podcast – Pushing Beyond the Obvious. Every single guest that I had on my show has been an expert in their own area and I have learnt something new from every one of them.

Practice:

What we also learn here is that without practice there is no growth or learning – irrespective of what we try to learn. So, practice we must. Knowing is not enough, doing is what helps us learn. Repeating what we have learnt is what helps us internalize our learnings. So, not only should we practice, but we should also repeat what we have learnt.

Falling and failing:

Zig Ziglar said it nicely when he said – "failure is an event, not a person". As long as we can identify with this quote, we don't have to worry about failing or for that matter falling. It is through this process of failing and falling that we learn and one day, suddenly we stop falling and failing and have learnt what we set out to learn.

This mindset is characterized by the motto:

Will not stop until I learn what I want to learn!

Putting in practice:

We can get into this mindset whenever we are in a situation where we want to learn a new topic about which we have no idea. Again, we will find it easier to learn to be in this mindset, if we are able to practice is this in a low risk setting.

Pick a topic that we have no idea about and explore if there is someone in your organization who could be your teacher or coach. If we can't find someone in person, let's look at the next best option, which is to enroll in a course (face-to-face or online). Then go about practicing and learning. Learn a new skill.

If you can't decide on which skill to learn, then learn to sketch or public speaking. Join a skill share course that can teach you how to sketch or speak publicly. These are life skills that are immensely useful, irrespective of your profession or vocation. Also, this also follows the same process that we have been talking about. The more you practice the better you get at it. You can actually see progress with your own eyes and it's easier to get feedback on your progress from the teachers as well.

The Philosopher's Mindset

Philosophers are known to ponder over things and try to find answers to some of the most basic questions that we as a race struggle with. Questions like "What is life's purpose?" or "Why do we do what we do?" or "What is right and what is wrong? Why?".

Self-reflection:

One of the key skills that philosophers possess is that they think deeply and debate with one another by explaining their own thinking. They are always exploring or rather they are always imploring. They are always looking inwards to find out what it is that we truly want and why it is that we truly want that. This ability to reflect is a super power in a world where everything is moving and changing so fast, in a world that is getting more and more superficial at everything (unfortunately, including relationships).

Thinking Critically:

Here is a great quote from Thoreau: "To be a philosopher is not merely to have subtle thoughts, nor even to found a school… it is to solve some of the problems of life not only theoretically, but practically." This constant questioning of belief's and thoughts is typical of philosophers.

They are able to focus and question our beliefs to get to the most fundamental issues in life and from there find answers. This ability to question beliefs until we reach to the most fundamental position and then find answers to these very fundamental questions is such a super power in a world where TL/DR (too long, did not read) is a phenomenon. This ability to stay with the thinking and focus deeply is so uncommon in a world where attention spans are shrinking to unprecedented levels.

Opposing Beliefs:

As they look inside of themselves for answers, they understand that there are a lot of dichotomies that are prevalent in nature. They understand that two belief's which seem to be opposing or contradicting each other could both be present, and both be true.

This understanding that two opposing beliefs can at the same time be true is an extremely valuable skill to possess. They understand that there is no such thing as absolute truth.

There is only subjective truth, my truth and your truth, and that both of them could be true at the same time, even if they both contradict each other. Most of the struggles in our lives are due to the fact that we believe that what we believe in is the only truth and that any other belief systems are no longer true.

This mindset is characterized by the motto:

> *I can be right and wrong at the same time!*

Putting in practice:

As with every other mindset that we have explored so far, it is important to practice this mindset in a low risk setting. We could look at something that we take for granted and try to put this to test. The best way to do this is to use the "5 why" technique, commonly used to do root-cause analysis.

For example, if you are someone who takes the same route to the office every day, start questioning this approach.

- Why do you take the same route to office every day?
- Did you decide on this route intentionally? Why?
- Did you decide to take this route because it is the fastest, shortest or the most scenic? Why?

- Do you like the predictability of the route or is it by habit or is it by default? Why?
- Do you really believe this? Why?

The simple act of asking why makes you go further and further into your own subconscious mind and tries to find the real reason for this action.

You could use the same technique and practice in a variety of scenarios. You could use this to question your own beliefs and habits.

Some of us have the habit of forming strong first impressions and rarely do we change these impressions about people who are in our lives. Questioning these beliefs and trying to understand truly what caused you to create that belief can be very fulfilling and at the same time insightful.

We can use the same mindset to question some business practices or processes that we follow to find out if they are still relevant or if they have lived passed their expiry date.

We can use the same mindset to question our own definition of the story of our lives. Why do we do what we do? Why is that? Why is that important? Do we really believe that? Why? This line of thought can lead us to come up with something that we truly value.

The Athlete's Mindset

One profession where the mindset can have a telling impact on how people end up performing is in the field of sports. While the mindset that we bring to our performance is important in every field of work, nowhere else its impact is seen so publicly than in the field of sports.

We have seen many athletes with great talent but with the wrong mindset flounder and vanish and athletes with average talent but with the right mindset flourish in almost all sports. This is the reason why almost all sports coaches treat mental conditioning with as much importance as physical conditioning. So much so, that good coaches will not tolerate even great players without the right mindset in their teams.

An athlete's mindset is a set of beliefs that enable them to do well in their respective sports.

Mind and Body:

This is probably one of the very few fields where everyone understands the importance of working on both our mind and body in order to succeed. They understand that training on one aspect and neglecting the other is a recipe for disaster. That is the reason why they are trained in both their mindsets and their physical capabilities. They understand (some of them intuitively and some of them intentionally) that body and mind are interconnected. When we work on one, we are automatically working on the other.

They will go about their physical practice irrespective of how they feel and once they start the physical work they realize that their feelings change to complement the physical work they are doing. As much as our mind influences our body, our body affects our minds as much, if not more.

Coach:

Irrespective of which sport you look at, the one thing that is a constant is the presence of a coach. The better the coach, the better the team or the individual athlete. The more the coach understands his coachee, the more he can personalize his/her attention. The presence of the coach plays a significant role in the athlete's overall success. Coaches help ensure that the athletes are working on every other aspect of an athlete's mindset.

Practice:

No athlete's day is complete without going through their practice. They practice every single day. They have a coach who helps them practice every single day. Their practice is not just repetition (while it is a very important part of practice) but also a learning session. They adjust their techniques, they find out what their flaws are and work on improving it. They find out what their strengths are and find works on improving that as well. They spend time visualizing their actual performance in the competition multiple times. They will explore what could potentially go wrong and try to put in place measures to counter such a scenario. They then actively practice these measures. They practice their plays so much that they become part of their muscle memory and hence become automatic when they find themselves in a similar scenario during their games.

Continuous Improvement:

Irrespective of how good the best athletes are, they are constantly looking to improve. They are always looking for ways to improve their game — both physical and mental. They know that if they don't constantly improve, they will not be able to stay in the game.

Champion athletes are constantly under the scanner and their game and game plan is being constantly studied by their competitors. So, they need to constantly learn and up their game to stay relevant and be able to compete at the same level. This creates an enormous importance for continuous improvement of their skills.

Humility:

Good athletes know that there will always be winners and losers. They will win some and lose some. This teaches them to stay humble. This humility is what drives them to continue to work on themselves and their games to stay on top.

The feedback from not practicing and not putting in the work shows is very quick in the field of sports. This ensures that athletes understand the importance of putting in the effort and the knowledge that no one can remain the champion forever provides for some humility.

While there are examples of many athletes who were not humble once they reached a level of success, history is proof that they don't last long in their fields once they lose their humility.

Vulnerability:

No other field shows our vulnerabilities as strongly and as prominently as the field of sports. Every athlete has vulnerabilities that can be exploited by their competition. One has to only look closer to find these vulnerabilities.

This constant focus on an athlete's vulnerabilities by their competition ensures that they themselves also look inward and identify these vulnerabilities and fix them before their competition can find them. This makes athletes one of the most self-aware sets of professionals that I know of.

<u>No Regrets:</u>

When it comes to game situations, good athlete's give it their all. They will not hold back any part of themselves. They unleash their training, their focus, their physical and mental toughness, their skills and the strength of their technique. There is no holding back. What this does is that there is generally no regret.

They understand that if their best is not enough, they will go back to identifying where they were found wanting (with the help of their coach) and will focus on improving that very thing by practice and constant improvement. Good coaches always tell their athletes to give their best performance possible under the circumstances and don't worry about anything else.

They focus on what they can control – their own practice sessions and their performances, the rest as they say, will take care of itself.

Sports is probably the only field that openly and publicly applauds and appreciates athlete's even if they lose, as long as everyone believes that they gave their everything and did not hold back. This is also the reason why we constantly see unknown athlete's come on stage and beat champions on their day.

This mindset is characterized by the motto:

Deliberate Practice is the womb where true champions are conceived!

Putting in practice:

This mindset can be put in practice in our everyday activities. Let's say, we have to routinely present to people as part of our job and is an important for your future growth in your organization. Then we can use this mindset to continuously improve this skill as an athlete would improve his skill at his own sport.

We could ask someone to coach us in this sport of presenting. This could be someone in your team, organization or even hire an external coach.

Show off your existing skills and ask for feedback and areas for improvement. Ask for your strengths. Ask for practical exercises that could help you improve both your strengths and your weaknesses. Then go out and practice it.

Find low stake situations and practice your game performance. You do that by volunteering to present your company strategy to new hires or join a toast master's club and present at their meetups.

Request your coach to be present during these presentations. If they can't be present, record these presentations and share the recordings with them and ask for their feedback. Constantly and continuously work on the skills. This a race with no finish line. The only time you stop is when you want to stop.

We can use the same mindset to practice our writing skills, or parenting skills or for that matter any skills.

The Actor's Mindset:

Another mindset that can prove to be extremely helpful is the actor's mindset. We are all actors whether we like it or not. We play different roles every single moment. We are parents, sons and daughters, aunts and uncles, nieces and nephews, bosses and employees, coaches and coachees. We change role as soon as the situation changes. We do it unconsciously and instinctively. Irrespective of what roles we play, we need to be authentic in our intentions and actions.

The way actors differ from us is that they are intentional about the roles they play and always know that they are playing a role and that this is not real. They possess the ability to lose themselves and instead bring out someone who is similar to them or completely different from themselves. They are able to do this as they are able to envisage themselves in their character's shoes. They can empathize with their character and move beyond that and actually become that character. They internalize the characters likes, dislikes, mannerisms, thinking, mental models, belief systems and hence are able to react to situations as if the character would react to that situation and not how they would react to the situation.

Observation:

Good actors are great observers. They look at the people closely. They study the characters around them, their mannerisms, their faults, their responses to typical situations and internalize these observations. They then mix and match these observations to weave a character that then becomes believable, with their own set of mannerisms and strengths and flaws. This is also the reason why so many of the actors are good mimicry artists as well.

Losing themselves:

We all possess this ability, but actors are able to hone this skill through practice and through self-reflection. They are able to use their own emotions to feed to their character's emotions. The most important skill that good actors possess that differentiates them from the pack and from us is their ability to lose themselves and become the character that they are playing.

Emotions:

At the core, acting is a show of emotions. So, actors need to emote. In order to be able to emote, they need to feel those emotions. Great actors feel the emotions of their character deeply and each one of these characters leaves a mark on their own psyche. Great actors are also able to also create a shell of their own, which is their true character and where they feel their own personal emotions.

This mindset is characterized by the motto:

> *I can be anyone I want to be as long as
> I know who I am!*

I think that a word of caution is necessary here. Even though I believe that an actor's mindset helps us transcend multiple limitations that we tend to put on ourselves, it is important to realize that if we are not authentic, honest in both intention and action, we will be found out and lose everything.

Putting in practice:

This is a skill that we can all learn and can prove to be extremely helpful when we are put in a completely alien environment. We practice this every single day in our lives already. We play the part of a parent, employee, boss, colleague, friend, son or daughter, counselor, guide, gardener, electrician and many more in different circumstances.

There are two things that can help us go a long way in helping us understand and learn the actor's mindset:

1. Active observation

2. Habit of getting in character

Active observation:

The best way to learn active observation is by practice and with practice we can get really better at this skill. To work on this skill, pick a specific time of a day or a specific location in your regular schedule. This is the time or place (even better if it is a combination of both) where you will learn to be an active observer.

The specific time could be your ride to your office in the morning or your weekly team meeting or a party that you attend. The specific place could be a train station or your office or a park where you go for a walk or any other specific place where you visit often.

Now, whenever you are in this place or at this specific time, you need to shut down all your devices and try to observe everything that is going on. If you are in a public space, pick out a specific person and observe what he or she does.

- What is he or she wearing?
- How are they walking?
- Are there any mannerisms that you can observe?
- Is there a pattern that you can notice?
- If they are close enough to you, notice how they sound or even smell?

- How are they interacting with their environment?
- Are they busy with their phone or are they interacting with their surroundings?
- If they are busy with their devices, what is their body language like? Can you find out what emotions they are experiencing?
- Just by looking at them from a distance can you guess what they are looking at on their phones?
- If they are not busy with their phones, what are they doing? Just by looking at them can you find out if they are happy, sad, angry or anything else? Why do you think they are feeling like that?

You don't need to do this for a long time. All you need to do is to practice this for maybe 10-15 mins a day. You could do the same with your spouse, child or colleagues as well. That will have the added advantage of you getting to know them much better and thereby helping in your relationship.

We will come back to this skill when we will talk about skills that can help us thrive in the next section.

<u>Getting in character:</u>

We all know that just the very act of the "clap" before filming a shot is to allow the actor to get into character. This is a cue to our brain that triggers the neurons that allow the actor to get into the skin (mind) of the character that they are playing. Our brains associate certain triggers with certain actions. That is how our brains work. For actors, it is the "clap".

We can use the exact same technique to train our brains to get into character. For example, you could use a specific object and tie its use or presence to signal to your brain to do a specific action.

Let's say, you want to play the part of a good parent and switch off your boss persona once you reach home. I know of people who will take bath as soon as they reach home and that could potentially be the signal to their brain to switch mode from being a boss to a parent. You could do the same thing by just wearing a special bracelet or a hat or changing into a specific dress or even as little as drinking a glass of hot milk (if that is the only time that you drink milk at home).

You can practice this by associating one object with a specific action that you want your brain to do. This is how habits are formed. More about habit formation in the skillsets section of the book.

How to use the different Mindsets:

It is well and good to know about all these different mindsets but there are still some questions that need to be answered before we can move to the next section:

- How do we know which mindsets are we currently operating in?
- How do we know which mindsets are good in which situations?
- And finally, how can we switch our mindsets on-demand?

Let's look at these questions in some detail.

Managing our mindsets:

The first thing that we need to do in order to actively chose the mindset that we want to be in, is to know our current mindset that we are operating under.

As with many things that are concerned with our brains, we generally prefer one way of thinking that is our default way of thinking. So, it is with mindsets. There is one default mindset that we generally operate under.

Before we even go ahead, please note that we might have a fixed mindset in a certain area of our lives at a specific time and a growth mindset in a different area of our lives. We should not assume that this is a fixed part of our personality.

For example, I have a growth mindset in almost all areas of my life, except when it comes to learning to swim or learn music. There, I seem to have a fixed mindset that you are either someone who could learn to swim or you can't. I think that you can either learn music or you can't. While I know that neither of them is true, I still struggle with it all the time. Maybe one of these days, I will be able to change my mindset over music and swimming as well.

The first step is for us to find out if we are in a fixed mindset or not. We can find this out simply by listening to our inner voice. If in response to a specific project or a situation, your inner voice is questioning your skills to navigate this current task/situation and reminds you of all the negative consequences that this specific action could lead you to, then you can safely assume that you are in a fixed mindset.

Once we find that we are in a fixed mindset and we want to change that to an appropriate growth mindset.

Carol Dweck clearly lays out a four-step process for us to bring about that change. I have added one additional step that can help us in a big way to the process laid down by Carol.

Learn to hear your fixed mindset voice:

This is the voice inside of you that asks you not to take up that challenge that could potentially lead you to experience failure. This the voice that is fearful of change. This is the voice that is happy with status quo and wants you to only do things that you are really good at. This is the voice that talks about all the shame that we will have to go through if we decide to challenge the status quo and fail.

Recognize that we have a choice:

We need to know that what makes us inherently human is that we are capable of taking a pause between a stimulus and our reaction to that stimulus, we can choose how to react to that stimuli. In any given situation, however bad it may seem, know that we always have a choice to look at it from a different lens. I remember a quote by Zig Ziglar, which helps me a lot. He used to say – "Remember, failure is an event and not a person!".

Identify the best growth mindset to be in:

Identify among all the options that we have practiced, which mindset will be the best one to adopt in this situation. At times, it could be an actor's mindset or a toddler's mindset or an entrepreneur's mindset or any other mindset.

<u>Talk back with a growth mindset</u>:

When you hear your fixed mindset talk to you, choose to reply to your inner voice calmly from the growth mindset. Internalize the mindset that we have identified in the previous step. You can use a learning language – I may not be sure to succeed in this specific project, but it is important for my future growth. Even if I fail, I would have learnt a lot or something like that.

<u>Take action</u>:

It is not enough to talk back to that inner voice. We need to take action that leads us to growth. The inner voice learns by observing the actions that we take. This inner voice constantly learns. The more this voice sees us take the risk and no harm coming, the more risk tolerant it will become. This inner voice will slowly learn and allow you to operate from a growth mindset, until, it detects a new threat, one that hasn't been experienced.

This also indicates that it is an ongoing process for all of us to identify if we are in a growth mindset or a fixed mindset.

Mindsets as habits:

In my practice, I have realized that this entire process of identifying which mindset we are in and then choosing the appropriate mindset is a difficult thing to execute. This requires a high level of self-awareness and the ability to have the right kind of self-talk, which I found very difficult when I started on my journey to explore and understand mindsets and how they work. I have also seen that some people are routinely able to do this easily and some people really struggle with this.

So, I wanted to find out what works really well. In the process, I discovered that our brain operates in a very specific way. Just like invoking a specific command in a computer program can start executing a series of steps that is pre-configured in the program, we can program our brain to set off a series of actions when prompted in a specific way. This is how habits are formed. We can use the same hack and trigger the right mindsets as and when we want them.

Another way to do this is by using the power of visualization. If you are a visual person (think in pictures) then it is much easier to visualize yourself acting out of a specific mindset. This serves as the trigger that can then put you in that mindset.

We all know that there are certain situations in our lives where a specific mindset would suit us the best. We can decide this in advance.

For example, I know that there is a specific skill that I need to learn at work, which is critical for my growth. I know that a toddler's mindset would work best. I now need to identify something that can trigger all the things that are part of the toddler's mindset.

This could be in the form of a physical object like a set of color pencil set around, which will serve the purpose of putting me in the toddler's mindset. This requires some amount of time, practice and plain repetition in order to get our brain programmed. But once done, the very act of having that set of color pencil around you, can put you in a toddler's mindset.

You could even use a specific dress or an accessory that you wear to trigger the mindset. You could also use some specific music to put yourself in a specific frame of mind. I know that a lot of writers and creative people use music or their environment as their trigger to get cracking at whatever they have programmed their brain for (writing, sketching, coding or anything else).

The trick here is that the more sensory inputs this trigger can give me, the better it is. It also requires at least some amount of practice and repetition in order for our mind to make this connection.

Our brain primarily learns from repetition and so it is critical. Also, we need to understand that we can only use a specific trigger for one set of activities. For every mindset that we want to get into, we need to have a separate set of triggers that each trigger the right kind of mindsets.

The easiest way is to start with a low stake situation, make it work through practice and repetition. Once we are comfortable with the process and believe that this is possible, we can then start looking at high stake situations and start applying this to those situations.

These triggers can help us put ourselves in specific mindsets almost instantaneously and their power, when used for our own benefit can be immense.

Skillsets

Every mindset requires us to use a set of skills that we have mastered in order for the mindset to be effective. In this section, we will see what skillsets we need in order to succeed in our lives and bring these mindsets alive.

Also, not all skills are created equal. There are some skills that we can call keystone skills or super skills that when mastered have a disproportionately large impact on our quality of life and enable everything else that we need to thrive.

Just like the first ripple in a calm body of water spreads out towards every corner of the water, these keystone skills serve us by enabling us to learn everything else that we need to learn to thrive in our environment.

I think that the below are the keystone skills that will help us thrive:

1. Learning to Learn
2. Staying Anti-Fragile
3. Being Data Smart
4. Being Emotionally Intelligent
5. Dealing with Artificial Intelligence
6. Being Persuasive

7. Being Creative
8. Avoiding Attention Traps
9. Being Curious
10. Building Habits
11. Story Telling

Let's explore each one of these skills as to why I think they are important and how does one go about acquiring these skills.

Learning to Learn

One of the most important skills that we all need to learn is the skill to learn anything new. This is a meta-skill. Just this one skill can have a significant impact on our lives. So, how do we learn, how to learn?

Scientific research tells us the following about how our brains function:

Our brain consumes a lot of energy in comparison to its relative size in our body. This leads it to find every possible way to conserve energy. This also means that it will almost always try to find a shortcut to doing what we want it to do. In some cases, this works really well for us and in some cases, it creates a lot of problems.

This is evident when we are taking the usual route to work or home and we are lost in our thoughts that we miss some of the scenery or even miss seeing the changing landscape and suddenly one day, we find that there is a new building up or a shop that used to be at a specific place is no longer there. This the brain trying to conserve energy and, in the process, blanking out every detail that is not immediately necessary for our drive to our destination.

We can also think of our brain like a vast network of highways that are all interconnected through various ramps and connecting roads. When we use a specific path more often than others, we are creating habits. Again, this conserves energy for our brain as we don't have to make too many decisions, which means less cognitive work for the brain.

Learning something new is easy if we can use what we already know to learn the thing that is new. This is the reason, metaphors and stories are a great way to learn new stuff. Using metaphors and stories in our learning process is like someone giving us the route using the routes that we already know. Learning then is about traversing the already known route to reach the destination that we want to arrive at.

Now, if we really want to learn how to reach this destination every time we want to, then we might have to use the route a few more times so that we can internalise the route. Once we are comfortable taking the route, we might even venture out to look at a faster or a shorter route to that same place. This is how learning happens. If we look at this process and break it down, it comes down to the following steps:

<u>Ignorance:</u>

This is the phase where we don't know what we want to learn. This is also the phase where we find ourselves almost every single day of our lives. We don't necessarily know exactly what we want to learn or that we even need to learn something.

Ignite:

Then comes along something or someone who helps us identify that there is some gap and that we need to learn something for us to achieve what we want to achieve. This is the time that we start thinking about learning something as it is needed. This can come about by us understanding our own limitations or can come by when someone shows us that there is a better, faster way to achieve what we want to achieve but we might have to learn this way.

Guidance:

This is similar to the phase where we now know the destination that we want to reach. Now, we need to find someone who knows the way or route to reach the destination. This could be a coach, mentor or a friend. They first tell us the route, which we may or may not be able to follow. Good teachers or guides then try to figure out what you already know and based on that they show you how you can reach the destination.

Practice:

Once you have the information, it is not enough for you to reach the destination. You might reach there once or twice, sometimes by chance, sometimes by following precise instructions that you got from the guide. You will then need to practice taking that route multiple times to get comfortable and confident of reaching the destination every time you set out for that destination. This is taking this route becomes a habit. You can do this without conscious thought.

Exploration:

If this level of knowledge is sufficient for our purposes, we can stop there. However, if we are looking to master the subject or destination, we need to go beyond just knowing how to reach from this origin to the destination. We need to learn how to reach that destination, irrespective of where we start. This needs us to do some amount of exploration. Sometimes we might succeed, sometimes we might get lost. However, it is critical that we continue to explore.

Knowledge:

Once we have done enough exploration, we then need to internalise what we have learnt from the journey. This internalisation is when we can say that we have acquired the knowledge of this route or subject or topic. Now you know everything that there is to know about how to reach that specific destination.

Inquisitiveness:

Once we have the knowledge, now we can tend to be more inquisitive. You can now start from wherever you are and explore the area further. You are now aware of different routes to take to reach the destination at different times of the day. You know the fastest or the shortest route to take at any specific time of the day as you have explored and learnt about this destination.

Mastery:

The last step in the process is when you are not only able to do this yourself but can be the guide who can help someone else do the same, just like your guide helped you reach your destination. That ability to understand the level of someone and then guide them in a way that they are able to learn and find their destination, is the time when you have reached mastery for that destination.

This process however is never complete. There are other destinations to reach and explore. There are other routes to explore and learn about. Ideally, this is a never-ending process, but we can stop when and wherever we want.

The same way, we can start this process when and wherever we want as well.

It doesn't require us to be a certain age or at a certain place or in a certain condition. All we need is the quest to learn and a guide or a master who can help in the process. And off we can go to start the process all over again.

Now, we also need to understand another thing about our brain, when it comes to learning. As with a lot of other things in our world, learning happens in two distinct phases:

- Focused phase: This is the time when we are deliberately trying to learn and practice. This is our conscious mind trying to learn new stuff.
- Diffused phase: This is the time when we are resting. During this rest, our sub-conscious continues to work on learning the new stuff. This is when learning takes route in our deeper mind.

So, if want to learn and internalise our learnings, we need to use both the phases of learning.

We first use the focused phase to create new pathways and practice these pathways. Then we use the diffused phase while resting to practice taking these pathways. Then we come back to the focused phase to explore if we have been able to internalise the learning. IF not, we continue to work on the focused phase to learn. Then we go back to the diffused phase to internalise the learning. This loop goes on till we are confident about having internalised the learning well.

This is the way we learn, irrespective of what we are trying to learn. So, it is critical to find a good master or guide who can understand us and our level of knowledge and accordingly guide us in our quest to learn the topic. This is the reason why professional athletes have coaches train them and leaders have business coaches to help them in their professional careers. Good coaches, mentors or teachers are crucial for our learning and continuous growth. We should always be on the lookout for such teachers.

Staying Anti-Fragile

Nassim Nicholas Taleb introduced the word "Anti fragility" in his book "Anti-Fragile". He argues that it is not enough to survive randomness, uncertainty and chaos. We can indeed thrive in this environment. In order to do so, we need to become anti-fragile. Anti-fragility is the opposite of fragility and gains from random events, chaos and uncertainty. The question we need to ask is the following:

> *Can we consciously train ourselves to become anti-fragile?*

I believe that we can learn to become anti-fragile. Then the question is how can we do that?

Expect & Embrace randomness:

One of the reasons anything becomes fragile is that it stops being able to handle randomness. If we as individuals stop being able to handle randomness, we become fragile as well.

So, the first thing for us to do in order to become anti-fragile is to expect and embrace randomness in our lives, maybe even introduce randomness in our lives. This allows us to not get flustered when a random event wrecks havoc around us. We know that we have dealt with random events in the past and have built up the confidence that we can deal with all sorts of random events. This is also where a YA mindset helps.

Let me share something that I experienced.

I was travelling to Germany for work and had a visa for a week. Once I reached Germany, I realised that I might have to stay for another week. So, with the help of one of my colleagues, I went to the foreigner's office in the city closest to the place that I was staying and applied for an extension of my visa. The process required us to fill out a few forms and then submit the filled-out forms and my passport.

So, we did exactly that and came back. A couple of days later, when I asked my colleague to check with the foreigner's office if my visa extension is done, he came back and told me that his contact at the foreigner's office told him that they are unable to process my request as they did not find my passport in the cover. They also agreed that they have a video recording of us dropping the passport and the filled-in forms in the drop box but said that they did not find the passport.

Somehow, the passport got lost.

Now, imagine this. I was in a foreign country, with an expiring visa and no passport. That would be a scary experience for most people. However, in my career, I had earlier travelled extensively in India, with no prior reservations, went to cities where I had absolutely no contacts and yet figured out how to find the right business partners and enrol them to become distributors for our products by paying us an advance deposit (in a trade where a 90 day payment cycle is the norm).

This past experience of travelling absolutely with no planning and coming across all kinds of random experiences (including a time when I had no money on me and had to ask a customer to come to a railway station to give me some cash, so I can pay the ticket checker for a confirmed reservation to the destination and buy tickets for the next leg of the journey, in days where there were no ATM's or mobile phones) had prepared me to deal with this experience without any panic.

I reached out to the Indian embassy in Frankfurt and was asked to visit the embassy the next day in order to explore other options I had. Next day, when I turned up at the embassy, I was told that it was a holiday at the embassy as it was a national holiday in India. This meant that there was no one at the embassy. I then had to tease out the mobile number of the consulate general from the security guard and call him to seek help. He then asked me to stay and asked an employee of the embassy to come back to the office and issue a temporary passport in my name, which I then submitted to the foreigner's office. Based on this document, they extended my visa and all was well until I came back home.

What happened when I came back to India and the struggle I had to apply and get a new passport is a story in randomness at play, but maybe, for another day.

I guess the point that I am trying to make here is that as with anything else, once you start experiencing a certain kind of experience, you start building the ability and the confidence to deal with similar situations. So, in order for us to be able to thrive in a world where random events are becoming to occur more frequently, we need to have the confidence that we can handle any such situation that might arise due to such random events.

Some examples of how I induce randomness in my life is as follows:

- I never take the same route to the office. Taking a different route to office introduces elements of randomness in my commute.
- I read books from different genres and different cultures. This introduces elements of randomness in my learning experience.

- I am open to taking unplanned trips.

We can create our own habits of how we want to embrace randomness and allow for surprises to spring up in our lives. The key here is that we allow for things to surprise us in small quantities, and gradually increase our ability to take in a surprising event and turn it to our advantage.

Stressors & our reaction to stressors:

Every system has its own set of stressors which create tension in the system. These stressors and how the system reacts or responds to these stressors indicates the relative strength or stability of the system.

As individuals, we are also systems and we also have stressors which impact the way we act. The first step in the process of building a better response to these stressors is to first identify them. We can do so by being aware of situations where we get stressed about something and we notice others around us not getting too much affected by the same situation. This situation or whatever preceded the situation is clearly a stressor that affects us.

Once we identify the stressor, we need to reflect on what about the stressor that creates such strong emotion within us. It generally is something from our past that we are holding on to and the stressor reminds us of that past. It usually is extremely difficult to identify this fragment of our past that is still hurting us. This is where we can use some help from family and friends and in some cases, even from counsellors.

It is important to identify this fragment of our past and deal with it so that it doesn't still hurt us. It is important to do this because these fragments are holding us back from making true progress in our journey to be the best that we can be. So, it is fine for us to take whatever help that we can get and address this, such that we are able to address this stressor.

Then we do the same with the next stressors. This is the same process we use when dealing and addressing phobias.

Domain Independence:

A lot of times, we become fragile when we start to identify ourselves very closely to a certain domain. This happens to all of us when our self-worth is dependent on this identity that we have created for ourselves. While being identified as an expert in a specific topic is a good thing, but not willing to work towards understanding a wide variety of topics in and around the topic in which we are already an expert is a cage that we build around ourselves.

And when the expertise becomes too narrow, we tend to lose sight of the big picture, which ultimately makes us fragile and any change in the big picture reality can leave us blind-sighted and we will not even know what hit us.

So, it is important for us to develop a "T" shaped personality. Someone is said to have a "T" shaped personality if they have developed expertise on a single topic and have a good enough knowledge about a few more topics. Someone who not only understands the topic in depth but also understands the big picture. Someone who is not only good at delving deep into a topic but also can go wide on relevant and sometimes even seemingly irrelevant topics.

The question then is how does one go about developing a "T" shaped personality?

One easy way is for us to expose ourselves to a variety of information sources (physiological, psychological & philosophical). In today's world, all the technologies are trying to use a predictive model to predict what you would like to eat, drink, watch; where would you go, whom would you friend or what would you buy. Instead of allowing these algorithms to predict our behaviour, we need to find a way to consistently beat these algorithms and find novel content to consume.

We can do so by being mindful of what we consume (physiologically, socially, psychologically and intellectually). We need to participate in multiple social networks with differing ideologies, practicalities and goals.

For example, I am deliberate in being part of multiple groups. Groups that want to network so they can make more friends, groups that come together to enjoy a good theatre performance, groups that enjoy reading books and discussing them, groups that are work related, groups that are diabetic (as I am one), groups that like travelling, groups exclusively for bloggers, as a podcast host, I bring on different kinds of people on my show, my reading list consists of all kinds of leanings and ideologies, which I publicly share on my social profiles. This keeps the algorithms from figuring out and creating a bubble around me.

Zoom:

Another way to go about developing the habit of zoom-in and zoom-out. This is a difficult skill to learn, but once we learn this, it becomes the way we start to think about anything that we deem to be important. This also allows us to ensure that we are rarely blind-sighted by the turn of events.

Zoom-in:

We are usually good at the zoom-in kind of thinking. We are taught in school to do root cause analysis using tools like fish-bone diagrams, 5 why method of questioning and more. The objective for zoom-in thinking is to understand the system up-close and to find out exactly what is happening. If we are studying a system, then finding out where is the system not working according to design or expectation. People who are good at this kind of thinking are typically in operational roles or problem-solving roles.

Zoom-out:

Once we have done the zoom-in thinking on the system or topic at hand, we need to then follow-it up with a zoom out thinking session. The objective for a zoom-out thinking session is for us to find out the big picture, find out the relationship between various elements of the system, trying to figure out why is the system behaving in a certain manner. Also, what kind of impact would a change in one part of the system have on the overall system. This kind of thinking is not normal and takes a lot of cognitive effort to do. People who are good at doing this kind of thinking usually are in leadership positions.

Once we are able to switch between zoom-in and zoom-out thinking, we are able to learn not only what is causing a specific effect and what effect will a change in one part of the system will have on the overall system.

Anything that can cause a fragile system to break has a larger impact than what is visible at the start. This is why most experts miss the significance of the events that go on to have a devastating impact on the system. The ability to zoom-in and zoom-out at the same time allows us to understand the overall impact a certain kind of action can have on any given system and so, we are able to see what others are unable to see faster and earlier.

Biomimicry:

Nature is the most anti-fragile system that we can come across. It thrives on chaos and constant change. There is a lot that we can learn from nature on becoming anti-fragile.

Multiple bets:

Nature always bets on multiple scenarios. This is the reason why there are so many varieties of anything that we find in nature. There are infinite varieties of fruits, flowers, animals, plants and even humans. In a way, nature knows that there will be some bets (species) that will not play out and some that will play out well. The fact is that nature itself doesn't know which bets will play out and which ones will fizzle. Hence the multiple bets.

Similar to nature, we also can place multiple bets that we think would play out for our benefit knowing fully well that some of them will fizzle and some of them will dazzle. As long as we have both kinds of bets, we should be on our way to becoming anti-fragile.

Interplay of systems:

Another thing that we can find in nature is that every system or an ecosystem is connected to all the other ecosystems in and around the original system. This interconnectedness is at the root of nature being so anti-fragile. Whenever a player fails in a natural ecosystem, there is someone already ready to take its place.

Irrespective of the system that we speak about, there is always an interplay of multiple systems at play. We need to identify the relationship and the interplay and to some extent even design these interplays in such a way that if something fails, there is something that can step-up and already take its place.

Balance:

Nature is balanced. You may call it the Yin and the Yang or the body and soul or any other such combination. There is always a balance in nature. Every time something impacts this balance, there is havoc all around and then nature figures out a way to get everything in balance yet again.

In our lives also, we should strive for such a balance. Every time we find that our lives are going out-of-balance, we need to realise that and do anything that brings the balance in our lives yet again. The ability to stay balanced is one of the most underrated ability that I know of.

So, in all, it is possible for us to learn from anti-fragile systems and incorporate the learnings into our lives and become anti-fragile.

Being Data Smart

We are now in a world which produces data in sizes that we can't even comprehend. As we produce so much data, we end up using the data in order to make almost every decision. Every organisation is looking for ways to gain insights from the data that they have already collected from their businesses and the data-set that is available through social media sites like Facebook or Twitter. We also share information about our heartbeat, the steps that we walk, how much do we sleep, when we sleep and how deep is that sleep.

There are two ways for the businesses to benefit from the data that they have at hand.

1. Use machines to find hidden patterns.
2. Use humans to ask questions of the data to gain insights.

Information → Insight using Machines:

There are a lot of people who are working tirelessly to teach machines to mine interesting patterns and learn from existing datasets. Machines are getting better and better at really processing large amounts of data and looking for patterns in the data that they can then spew out. Once these patterns are detected, we need someone who can look at the patterns to gleam if there is something that we can do as a result of the pattern to help the business in their goals.

In some cases, this will also be done by a machine but at least for the foreseeable future, most organisations would still want some human touch before they can allow machines to make changes to their business based on these patterns that they have found. They will still want someone to look at the patterns or insights gained from the patterns and do some further analysis and decide whether it makes sense to continue to investigate the pattern.

The key questions, in that case, are going to be the following:

1. Is this a pattern that will occur regularly or at a certain period of time or when there is a specific trigger to this pattern or to put it in simpler terms, can this pattern be reliably reproduced when needed or will occur at a predictable pace?
2. Now that we know this pattern exists, what can be done as a result of knowing this pattern?
3. Once we list down some actions that we can take based on the insight, what would be the reaction to this action. This is where we need to be able to use predictive models (these are computer programs that can compute potential outcomes if we are able to give the conditions) and see

potential outcomes of the actions. In some cases, we can use standard predictive algorithms, but in most cases, these algorithms would need to be written or at least standard algorithms will need to be adapted to our needs.
4. We then analyse the results of the predictive algorithms and decide if any of the specific actions can be implemented in the business.
5. Once this is done, then we can again look at the data and use machines to figure out what would be the perfect way to pilot test the action, before we go ahead and implement it business wide.

In some organisations, due to the nature of the business, they can do all of this without human intervention, but such organisations are few and far in-between. Most organisations for the foreseeable future will still need some human intervention before they can allow the machines to make a decision and implement it all by itself.

Information → Insights using Humans:

The second way to get a lot of value from the large volume of data is to use the innate ability of humans (called intuition) and their understanding of business and human nature.

In this scenario, humans will look at the vast data set that businesses collect and look at the data and ask intelligent questions, that can bring out interesting insights, that can then be tested and acted upon.

The key thing here is the ability ask intelligent questions.

In order to do so, we need to inherently understand the source of the data, in some cases understand the core businesses to understand the structured data that a business generates or the platform which generated the data along with the context in which the data was generated. Based on this understanding humans can use inherently human abilities like empathy and intuition to ask intelligent questions of the datasets.

The only difference between gaining insights from information using humans and machines is that in one case, the insight arrives from a human and in the other arrives from a machine. All the other steps still remain the same. You still need to validate the insight and its relevance in a specific situation. You still need to be able to convert the insight into an action that you can initiate in your business. You still need to be able to use predictive models (human or machine based) to predict the reaction you might get once you implement the action. You still need to pilot it in a contained environment to validate your predictions, before going all in and implementing the change in the business.

Skills that you need in this environment:

Identify the right data:

The first thing we need to be able to do is to identify the right data to work on (among the ocean of data) that we generate. This will generally come from the facet of the data generating world that we want to work upon.

Getting comfortable with data:

We need to be able to train ourselves to look for data in everything that we do. There is some information that is available somewhere that can make it easier. This information can also be some anecdote that we have heard someone share. Irrespective of whether we think this is a good thing to do, most organisations will work on the premise that validating data is needed in order to make any change at all.

Dealing with data:

We need to be comfortable looking at vast sets of data and mining the data through statistical tools. So, we need to learn some form of statistical tools. At least some basic working knowledge of statistical concepts and the ability to work with these statistical tools will be needed to do well in this world.

Dealing with predictions:

We need to be able to at least understand what predictive models are and what some of the most often used predictive models good for. So, a basic understanding of predictive models is necessary. It is important to also understand the logic used by a specific predictive model so that we understand the insight gained by using a predictive model.

Dealing with insights:

We need to be able to understand the insight that we gain in its original context. This means that we need to be able to understand the context in which it was generated or the business landscape and how different parts of the business interacts with each other.

Dealing with prediction of actions:

We need to be able to have enough information and knowledge of the business and human tendency to understand how people will behave in a specific situation and how they might reach if the situation is changed by introducing new elements or taking away some elements.

Data can lie:

We need to understand that there is an inherent bias in us that will tend to make us only look at the data that validates our insights. We need to be wary of this facet of data and try to overcome this bias by systematising the way we look at the data, ie, we consciously go look for data that could contradict our view point before we take a decision. This one step, if not done well, can derail the entire data driven decision model in an organisation and in some cases, the organisation itself.

Once we understand the power and limitations of data within the context in which the data was collected, we can then design experiments and use this to continuously improve our ability to gain insights from the data and thereby create new possible actions based on these insights.

Being Emotionally Intelligent

I think that there are three levels of intelligence in humans:

Intellectual intelligence:

This is all about understanding things as they are and the ability to make sense of the world around us. This is the cognitive intelligence or the ability to comprehend complex systems and subject matters that require us to use logic. This level of intelligence allows us to excel as an individual.

Emotional intelligence:

This is all about understanding our own emotions and showing empathy to understand the underlying emotions of people around us from their actions. This level of intelligence allows us to excel not just as individuals but also excel while working with others.

Spiritual intelligence:

This is all about understanding the true reason for our existence as spiritual leaders talk about. At this level it is about perspectives about humans as a race and trying to understand the reason for our existence and the relationship that we have with fellow humans and everything else around us. This level of intelligence allows us to go beyond our immediate needs and excel not just as small communities (or teams) but as an ecosystem of things (living and non-living).

<u>The Importance of Emotional Intelligence:</u>

While we all strive to become intelligent at the highest level, it requires us to first become emotionally intelligent by understanding ourselves and our actions better. When we have done that, we then need to build the ability to understand the base emotions that drive the actions of people around us.

This ability to understand and deal with emotions – both ours and those of people around us, is in a way a super-power that all of us can possess.

As we have discussed earlier in the book, humans are essentially emotional beings. We have observed that we mostly decide on almost everything based on our emotions and then try to use logic to justify or explain our decisions. This is also the root cause of so many cognitive biases that have been chronicled by behavioural scientists from around the world. This is also the reason for so many things that we see around the world that are extremely difficult to explain using logic.

The question now is for us to thrive in the world that we are moving in to, we need to be able to not only diagnose and be in control of our own emotions, but also be able to feel empathy towards others around us, thereby understanding their emotional state and acting accordingly.

The question then is the following:

> *How do we become more empathetic and emotionally intelligent?*

As with everything else, we need to practice empathy in order to become better at being empathetic. We can start small and start with self.

Understanding Self:

Practice 1: Meditation:

The first step in developing our emotional intelligence is for us to get better at recognizing our emotions and biases. One way that I have seen people get better at doing this is through meditation. At first, we start with guided meditation. There are many mobile applications and websites which offer guided meditations. You could even find an ashram where groups come together, and a teacher helps the group to meditate by guiding them through the process of meditation. This is simple, but not necessarily easy.

Practice 2: Mindfulness:

The second thing that we can do to understand ourselves and our emotions better is to become mindful of them. This is as simple as setting up an alarm for every hour of the day and when the alarm goes off, take a deep breath and ask ourselves, what are we feeling (emotions like being bored, angry, happy, sad, lonely, joyous, ecstatic, frustrated, etc). The more we practice this, the easier it gets and the better we get at detecting our very own emotions.

Practice 3: Self-Reflection:

The third practice that will help us in understanding ourselves and our emotions is the art of self-reflection. Set aside some time every day for self-reflection. We don't need a lot of time, even about 10 mins will do.

Sit in a comfortable position and take a few deep breaths. Then think about the day that has passed and try to identify the most important moments of the day. This could be some decision that you made, some interaction you had with someone important or some strong emotion you felt. Once you have identified these important moments, try to reflect on what you were feeling at that moment.

Then think about why did you feel the way you felt? Then think if you could have been better off feeling or acting in a different way than you did? If not, congratulate yourself on being true to yourself.

If you think you could have responded at the moment differently, think about what would have been a better way to respond? Think of the same situation playing out again in your mind and imagine you responding to this situation, now, with the better way that you have identified. Repeat this for every important or critical moments that played out in the day.

Once you do this on a regular basis, you will come to see some patterns in your behaviour that points to specific tendencies or biases that you were earlier unaware of. We can then decide what we do with this information. We might still decide not to do anything at all, which is fine as well, or we might decide to change something or break a pattern of reactions to certain stimuli. We can do the same via self-reflection and visualising the kind of change we want to bring about in our feelings/actions in the given situation.

<u>Understanding others:</u>

Just like the only way to grow a tree is to first plant the seed, then water it and allow it to sprout, then take care of the sprout, until it evolves into a tree, we need to first be able to understand ourselves and our emotions better, before we are able to understand others.

The process is the same three steps – meditation, mindfulness and reflection. This time, we do this with people around us. Once you have tried to understand your feelings in a given situation, you then try to think about and understand the feelings of others in the same situation. You try to put yourself in their shoes and think from their perspective. What did they see, hear or feel in that situation? Given the baggage they carry around, what does that translate to? What were they trying to accomplish? Why?

One thing that I have realised based on my experience is that most people don't walk around thinking about harming or hurting others around them. They don't want to make stupid decisions or be stubborn for the sake of being stubborn. They usually have a point of view that makes them believe that what they are doing is the right thing to do. They might fail to see your point-of-view or perspective.

Knowing this, I have started to give people the benefit of doubt and approach people who seem to be exhibiting behaviour that we think is not the right one with curiosity. Curiosity to understand the perspective that makes them think that their actions are right and that our position is flawed. Once I started giving people the benefit of not being wrong, I realised again and again that in most situations, there are multiple perspectives and at times two diametrically opposing views may both be true. This understanding has allowed me to resolve conflicts and work much better with people. IT can do the same for you as well.

Once we understand their perspective, we can gradually progress to more deeper questions like – What drives them? What is their ultimate goal? Are they aware of what they are doing and why? Are they aware of what effect their actions are having on the people around them? Is there something you could do to help this person? And when we are able to do this, we are able to connect with that person on an emotional and intellectual level. This one skill can have a disproportionate amount of impact on our effectiveness.

Mirroring:

It is not every time that you will have time and information about someone whom you need to empathise with. So, in situations where you don't know the person too well or don't know his or her emotional state too well, but would like to connect with them, we can put in use one of our hidden talents to good use – mirroring neurons.

As humans, we all have subtle signs when we interact with people that they can pick up. According to research done by neuroscientists, mirror neurons in the brains of mammals enable us to mimic each other's behaviours in unconscious ways. This is the reason why yawns are contagious, so is stress and happiness. This is the basis for our ability to empathize with others. We also know that feeling emotions lead to physical sensations and inducing physical sensations can lead us to feel the emotions as well.

So, if we want to empathise with someone whom we don't know much about, we can simply, consciously try to mirror them and their body language and we will automatically start feeling the way they are doing. For example, we can try to match our breathing to theirs, we can mirror their body language (lean back if they are leaning back, cross our arms if they are crossing their arms, etc).

The very act of these physical actions has the potential in us to feel the emotions that they are feeling. The only thing that might hinder this from happening is if we are from totally different cultures and if the physical body language means different things in the different culture. So, as long as we are aware of this limitation, we can use the power of mirroring to quickly empathise with anyone, whom we may or may not know much of.

Dealing with Artificial intelligence

We are living in a world where we will have an ever-increasing number of artificially intelligent beings (bots). Every one of us need to understand how susceptible we are to the powers of Artificial Intelligence and more so to the influences of those who control these bots.

With persuasive technologies and cognitive computing and cognitive intelligence, we will see a barrage of bots that will act, speak and respond like humans do. There are already early indications that in some part of the worlds, humans already are able to crave and form deep relationships with bots. It turns out, it doesn't matter if the other partner is a human or an AI bot, we still seek company and yearn for someone who can understand us and listen to us. When humans stop doing this (as we are all getting busier with our own devices), bots can take over this role. What worries me in this scenario is that these bots are created by commercial organisations that are expected to create profits for themselves and their shareholders and the bot is a black box. We have no idea what the bot has been programmed for (by humans) and how will it evolve (by itself) thereby making us vulnerable to both good and bad influences by bots.

While regulation and standard ethics committees, corporate responsibilities and open artificial intelligence API's could be a part of the solution, it is still in our best interest that we are aware of this challenge and are ready to tackle it. Tristan Harris is leading a movement called Time Well Spent to bring this issue to the forefront of public consciousness.

I believe that it is not just Artificial Intelligence that will continue to evolve with time, but we as a race will also continue to evolve along with this intelligence. The question to ask is will our evolution be as quick as the evolution of AI? While this is a natural process and will continue to happen, we have a responsibility for ourselves to not just wait for the evolution to happen but take charge of our own individual evolution in our own lives.

How to deal with AI effectively:

There are a few things that we can implement in our lives which will help us in dealing with AI that is beneficial to us. These are the same things that can help us have healthy and fruitful interactions with our friends, family and colleagues as well.

Intention:

One of the most important things that we need to start with is to have a clear intention. Clarity on what we want from our interaction with the bot or with a human. Knowing what we want from an interaction ahead of time, primes our mind to be focused on what we want and thus helps us get what we want and stop there.

Similarly, we need to try and understand the intention of the bot in our interaction. Is the bot designed to sell to me or service me or anything else? What human biases does the bot have inbuilt? Every bot is being created by humans and their biases can and will get transferred to the bots that they are creating.

For example, there are biases built into simple things like an automated tap. The design of the tap is such that when we bring our hands below the tap, it needs to open and spew out water. People have shown that the same tap works without a hitch when a white person uses it and doesn't work at all when a person of colour tries to use it. When biases can enter in such low-tech stuff, I am sure that biases will enter into bots as well. We need to be intentional about finding out the bias that has been pre-built in the bots, so that we can deal with it accordingly.

Attention:

Once we know what we want to get out from our interaction with a bot, we need to pay attention to our behaviour and that of the bot to ensure that we are not being sucked into a wormhole that we don't want to go into. This ability to pay attention to the interaction and stay focused on the intent of the interaction can help us remain in control of these interactions.

Why is this so difficult:

The reason why it is difficult to do this is that it takes a lot of mental energy to first identify the intention and then focus our mental energies to pay attention.

Our body is built to conserve or optimise energy spent and so will always take a shortcut if there is one available. We need to train ourselves and our body, so it learns that it is important to spend this energy. What we need to understand and internalise is that this ability to identify the intention for an interaction and pay attention to the same during the interaction is a skill that we can learn with practice. With enough practice this skill can become a habit. Once this becomes a habit, we don't need to spend the same amount of energy to continue to do this as this becomes second nature to us.

Avoid bubbles:

One of the limitations that the early versions of AI is that they will tend to create bubbles around us. As most of the AI recommendation engines will use our current actions and likes and interactions online (and maybe offline), they will continue to serve same or similar kinds of stuff and thereby put us in a bubble where we will tend to become oblivious of everything else around us. This is what leads to polarisation in our thinking and actions.

Once we are aware of this tendency, we can create counter measures to try and ensure that we don't end up living in a bubble created by AI.
Some action I take in order to ensure that i am able to counter the AI's tendency to create bubbles are:

Train the AI:

We are constantly training every AI system that we interact with by our actions, either intentionally or otherwise. So, since we are anyway training the AI, we may as well train the system such that it benefits us more than the lords that the AI system serves.

- I consistently like and share opinions on all three sides of the spectrum (Left, Right and center) on any topic.

- I consistently like and share articles and posts on a variety of topics (religion, politics, books, philosophy, technology, design, creativity, sales, marketing). You can see this in action if you follow me on any of my social channels.
- I consistently create content (blog, podcast, videos, online courses, tweets, etc) on a variety of topics as well.
- I consistently explore different genres of music, movies and documentaries.
- I consistently avoid taking the bait of recommendations by AI systems. The way the system learns and provides us recommendations is by learning from our actions (responses to their recommendations). By not responding to the recommendations, I am taking away crucial information that the system needs to put me in a bucket. I may still watch a movie recommended by the AI system but by responding to the recommendation but by searching for the movie directly and accessing it from thereon.

We will be profiled by AI, whether we like it or not. However, it is in our best interest to ensure that we are in control of what kind of profile do we end up in the AI system. The operative word in all the above actions that I take to train the AI system is consistency.

The AI system will continuously evolve and make it easier and easier for us to respond to its recommendations. They will take away all the friction from our interaction with the AI system. What we need to do is to re-build that friction in our every interaction with the AI system. This way, we are in control more often than not, thereby enabling us to game and benefit from the AI system rather than the other way around.

Relationships:

There are already instances where we are seeing that businesses are able to create AI systems that are able to mimic what we need from our friends and family. We have also seen that in the situation where we lack fulfilling relationships in our life, we can very well explore relationships with AI systems. This is already happening as I write this book.

So, in order to truly deal with AI systems effectively, we need to be our best human self, that we can be. We need to fulfil our need for fruitful relationship amongst humans rather than go looking for the same in AI systems. This means that we need to become more human than we have ever been and building fruitful and meaningful relationships with our friends, family and colleagues is much more critical today than it has ever been.

Again, we can see the importance of emotional connection and empathy in a world that we will be inhabiting.

There are significant benefits that bots and AI bring to our lives. Also, we can't stop the progress that science and entrepreneurs make by using the AI, which means that whether we like it or not, AI is going to become larger and larger part of our lives. And it will get better and better at controlling our behaviour.

So, we need to be intentional about when we leverage this strength of smart AI to help us become better version of ourselves and when we stop allowing it to affect our behaviour.

Being Persuasive

The ability to persuade others is a super-skill. Robert Cialdini wrote about the universal principles of influence in his seminal work with the same title. He said that there are six principles at work when it comes to influencing:

1. Reciprocity
2. Liking
3. Authority
4. Social Proof
5. Scarcity
6. Consistency

Each one of these principles builds on certain inherently human traits and are not different from what most religious scriptures talk about.

Reciprocity:

This is an inherently human trait. If someone treats you well, we tend to treat them well. If someone treats you badly, we either treat them badly as well and if the social circumstances don't allow that due to difference in status, we tend to keep this in mind and respond in kind whenever we get an opportunity.

Physiologically this is true as well. We all have something in our neural system called as mirror neuron. The job of these mirror neurons is to mirror the action of the person we are interacting with.

In social interactions among peers, we can notice this all the times. When One person leans back or forward, the other follows; when someone yawns, the other follows; even the breathing tends to move towards becoming similar (shallow or deep). The language tones follow as well - someone raises their voice, the other responds.

The same thing happens with emotions as well. When you meet someone, who is angry and frustrated, the anger and frustration within us get activated as well. When we meet someone, who is tranquil and happy, we start to feel these emotions as well.

This is the reason why holy men are sought after by masses, because by them being calm and patient, they inspire the same feeling in their followers. This is also extremely evident in people who work for a manager for some period of time taking on the mannerisms of the manager.

While this is a typical response of the mirror neurons, we can control them with practice. This means that instead of being controlled by the emotions and actions of the people around us, we can lead their emotions if we are calm and in control of our own self. So, for example, we are in a situation where tempers are frayed, and we enter with a calm mind and in control of ourselves, we can have an impact on everyone else and get them to start the process of calming down. If we want the people around us to feel happy, we can do so by being happy first. If we want people around us to feel hurt, we can do so by feeling hurt first.

This is a primal form of influence that each one of us has the ability to exert over people around us. Once we understand this and practice our ability to control our emotions inside out, we start building the ability to influence others around us.

Liking:

It is no surprise to learn that it's easier to be influenced by people whom we like and vice versa. There are many ways to become liked among the community that we want to influence. However, the best way to be liked is to like others and like them authentically.

The fastest way to get someone to like us is to pay them an honest compliment. The second fastest way to get someone to like us is to listen to them and their story with interest.

So, in order to be able to pay someone an honest compliment, we need to be open to look at them and their full personality with the focus of finding something that we can appreciate and pay a compliment about. This is not the natural behaviour of our psychology and physiology.

The first thing we notice when we meet someone whom we don't really know well is to make a snap judgement about the person on one question – opportunity or threat and to do so, we need to first look at potential threat and the absence of threat is construed as potential opportunity. So, even when there is a lot to be appreciated, the thing we notice first is always what is wrong (threat).

We need to work on ourselves to stop this from happening automatically (at least when we want to influence someone) and take charge of the process to rather look for the positives. It takes effort and practice to be able to build this ability to by-pass the natural behaviour of our brain and to create a new habit of focusing on the positives first (at least in some situations to start with).

There is enough literature and research on the art of listening to others. However, there is one thing that stands out. In order to listen to others, we need to first stop talking, not only to the person we are trying to listen to but to ourselves, in our minds.

Some ways that I have become better at listening are:

1. Talk to yourself and tell yourself that you will listen more and deeply. Do that just before you enter into a conversation. This sets you up for listening better.
2. Breathe. Decide to take a deep breath before speaking. This gives you a couple of seconds before responding. This couple of seconds might seem like an eternity to you and a minuscule amount of time to whom you are listening to.
3. Practice being comfortable in silence. If there is one thing that I learnt from my first mentor, it was how uncomfortable silence can be in a conversation. People will do anything to remove silence from a conversation. If you can bring in silence, people will open up and share stuff that they never planned on sharing.
4. Be interested in what the other person has to say. It shows. People can immediately tell if someone is interested in what they say. And when they see genuine interest, they feel good and share much more than they planned on sharing.
5. Practice listening to all kinds of sounds. You could be listening to music or a coffee machine or even birds chirping. The key is not to do anything else

while listening. This is low stakes training to learn to listen. Also, as there is nothing being said, there is nothing to respond either. This act of pure listening helps us increase our ability to listen.

Authority:

You can influence people when they consider you an authority on the topic that you want to influence them on. This authority could be your own, based on your experience and skills or it can be authority by association. This means that you get authority by being associated with someone who has authority or being seen with people who have authority (real or perceived). This means that while we continue to build our authority with experience, we can still be able to use this authority-on-loan to influence people.

By the mere association with people who have authority, we can claim authority as well. This is the reason why the secretaries of powerful people are as powerful as their bosses. This is also the reason why people close to powerful people automatically get feel more powerful than they really are.

Social Proof:

Social proof is the reason you will find authors and bloggers mention that they contribute to Forbes or HBR or Inc. This gives them authority on the topic by association and social proof. Even if you have never read a word that the person has written for any of these publications, the mere mention that they are contributors for these publication gives them the authority on their topic as far as we are concerned.

This is also the reason why published authors are given and feel more authority on the topic of their book, even if they may not be the most authoritative voice on the topic. By having contributed on publications that are considered the best and having stringent measures for allowing anyone to write to them, they offer social proof that anyone who contributes to these magazines must be an authority on the topic. Why else would HBR or Forbes carry their words?

Scarcity:

People typically want more of things that they have less of. They want more money. They want more time. They want more attention. If we can help them in getting more of what they want, we can exert influence on them and their behaviour. If we control a scarce resource that everyone wants, we can become influential. This is the reason why we pay hundreds of thousands of dollars to someone to come and address a gathering of people. They and others around them consider their time and attention as scarce resources. This is exactly the reason why something that is rare to find becomes expensive.

This principle also rides on one of our inherent biases – loss aversion. Losses hurt us more than gains can give us pleasure or happiness. This means that one way to influence people is to show them what they stand to lose if they act in a way than if they acted in a different way. The whole insurance industry runs on this principle.

Consistency:

This is probably the easiest way to build influence and persuade people. We underestimate the power of consistency. This is the same principle by which flowing water can move mountains and make way for itself.

Getting up every day or week or fortnight and writing a blog post (podcast or a video) on a specific topic is a good start to building authority and influence on the topic. Over time people come to expect your blog (podcast or a video) and will start treating you as though you are an authority on the topic, even if you don't write anything original.

There are a lot of ways for us to build influence over others. The easiest and the fastest way to do so is by ensuring that we keep the best interest of the people we want to influence or persuade. This is the single most important thing for us to remember. There is a difference between influencing people and taking them for a ride. People will never forget or forgive you if you take them for a ride.

Influencing happens when your interest and your subject's interests converge at some point.

Being Creative

Being able to be creative on-demand has always been a super-power. There is a lot of literature about creativity and how to become creative. There are countless books on this topic. There is also a lot of debate about whether creativity is a skill and if can it be learnt and learnt by adults.

My personal opinion is that we are all inherently creative. If you are able to tell a lie, you are creative. Every one of us is immensely creative in a specific way in a specific situation. The seed of creativity is there in each one of us and is flowering in some form or factor. It may or may not be flourishing in our work environment.

Just like a seed has the inherent ability to become a tree and provide not only for every other living being around it, but also to pro-create for itself, each one of us has the inherent ability to become immensely creative not just for our own selves but also for everyone around us.

So, what is needed for our creativity to flourish?

The Right Environment:

Just like a seed needs a specific kind of environment for it to sprout, our creativity also needs a specific kind of environment. We need to believe that we have the seeds of creativity inside of us.

Just like a seed needs a nurturing environment for it to sprout, our creativity needs a nurturing environment for it to flourish. We need an environment where we are encouraged to express our creativity. We need an environment which is non-judgemental about our art. We need an environment which is full of creativity. We need an environment where we are not only encouraged to express our creativity but are also asked to encourage creativity in others as well.

The Right Inputs:

Once you have the right environment, a seed needs the right care. It needs the right level of sunlight, water, fertiliser, etc. Similarly, our creativity needs the right inputs for it to flourish. Creativity is the result of mixing and mashing of existing ideas into new ideas or new ways of expressing an old idea. So, in order for us to be creative, we need a constant stream of creative endeavours or expressions fed into us. The more creative ideas we feed on, the more creative we allow ourselves to become.

The Right Skills:

Just like a seed already knows everything it needs to know to grow into a tree, we all already know everything we need to know to be creative. All we need to now do is to look inside of us and tap into our creative self.

This can be done by allowing ourselves to practice our creativity and express ourselves. This is what we mean by practicing our craft. This is what we mean when we know that it is important to not only practice our craft but also to continue to learn as we go along depending upon where we are in the scale of novice to an expert.

The Right Care:

A sprouting seed is probably at its most vulnerable self in its entire life, so is budding creativity. If we don't protect it and give it the right environment and allow it to blossom into a tree, the potential of the seed goes waste. Same it is with creativity. We need to express our creativity in a protected environment first and then gradually start allowing ourselves to become more vulnerable with our expressions.

The Fruits:

Just like a seed (that fruits) that has turned into a tree is now able to give back to its environment in every way possible, so can we start giving back to our environment creative ideas as and when needed. Once we have grown ourselves into the tree (have confidence, know our craft and have been expressing our creativity in more and more vulnerable ways) we are able to bring out creative ideas on-demand.

The Ecosystem:

Just like every seed has to grow into a specific tree, which has a specific function in nature, so do each one of us grow into unique individuals who have a specific role to play in our worlds. Just like a whole bunch of different trees (and plants) make an ecosystem, a whole bunch of us make an ecosystem as well.

The true strength of our creativity surfaces when we function together as an ecosystem (or team) and not just as individuals as this brings about a whole new level of creative expression.

Having said this, I do believe that there are a lot of things that we can do to increase our ability to be creative on demand. We can create practices and routines in our lives that will allow us to be creative on demand. Some of the routines that have been very helpful to me are presented here.

Use Principles of Chemistry:

A lot of times creativity is like chemistry. You mix up certain elements or compounds and you get new compounds with completely different properties from the initial ingredients. So it is with creativity.

You need to have a lot of ingredients to select from. You pick two or more unlikely ideas, mix and match them, shake them up a bit and you have a novel idea. The more ideas that you have up your sleeves, the more novel ideas that you can come up with.

What this means is that:

- You need to read a lot of different sources about a lot of different stuff.
- You seek out ideas in different fields.
- You build a network of people who are very different from you.
- You are part of different social groups who hold different things close to them.
- You make note of interesting ideas as you come across them and save them somewhere you can access them at a moment's notice.

There are a lot of tools that are available today that enable you to do just that. Find what works for you and use it regularly and rigorously.

Use Frameworks:

There are a lot of frameworks that are available today that can help us in being creative on demand. One such framework is what is called as SCAMPER. This is an acronym.

- S - Substitute
- C - Combine
- A - Adjust
- M - Modify
- P - Put to Other use
- E - Eliminate
- R - Reverse

There are many more frameworks (Triz, Anti conventional Thinking, etc) that are available for creative ideation. You can pick and choose the one that works for you in a given situation. All of them work really well, as long as you use the framework as you are supposed to use them.

Seek inspiration:

Fonts for computers were inspired by the age-old calligraphy that one Steve Jobs had learnt while he was in college. The Star Wars series of films were inspired by Japanese films by Akiro Kurusowa and their culture. The legendary design of the iPod was inspired by either the Braun T3 pocket radio or the Bang and Olufsen's BeoCom 6000 phone (depending on whom you want to agree to), but the design similarities are unarguable.

As you can see, some of the most creative works that you will ever come across are a result of someone getting inspired by something so much so that it leads them to create something that is truly creative. Finding inspiration from some work of art or otherwise and adding to it our very own individualism leads us to create something unique. The key is to take the inspiration and then make it our own.

Use your Body:

One of the things that neuro-scientists have known now for a long time is that every time we are able to pump blood to our brains, our ability to connect disparate things and come up with original ideas increases. So, before you want to be creative, go out for a brisk walk, do some exercise or have sex even. Anything that can pump blood through our body and to our brains. Apart from all the physiological & psychological benefits that exercise provides us, it is also great for us to be in the mindset to create.

Reframe:

Everytime we want to be creative and solve problems, we think of the problem and the solution being in the same frame of reference. The moment we are able to change that frame of reference, we open up a lot more possibilities for creative solutions.

One way to do this reframe is by increasing or decreasing levels of abstraction. You can get more abstract or more definite. Depending upon the level of abstraction, we can re-look or re-define the problem or solution.

Another way to reframe is by changing the point of reference. So, for example instead of thinking about creating a product that is easy to produce and distribute, you now think about creating a product that is easy to consume. This change in the reference point can completely create a new series of creative insight and ideas. This is also the reason why introducing constraints unleashes new ideas.

Practice:

The ability to create creatively is like any other skill. It takes practice and patience to increase our skill levels, to progress from being an apprentice to becoming a master. Not any kind of practice but what Anders Erickkson refers to as "Deliberate Practice".

Deliberate practise is when you pick an important area where you need to improve and focus on that area until you become proficient. You continue to do this to continually improve from your practice. This requires you to find a coach or a mentor who can help you learn from both their personal experience and from his learning from others' experiences. Once we have a good coach, our chances of becoming really good in that field then depend on our commitment to excellence.

So, keep practicing (deliberate practice) your creative muscles every day and have patience. You will get really good at it.

Avoiding Attention Traps

We live in a world where some very smart people are trying very hard to ensure that we pay attention to stuff that they are creating. They are using all sorts of behavioural insights to first hook us to their products or services and then make us keep going there for more. They then use this mechanism to build habits that may or may not be what we want in our lives.

What this means is that we need to smarter than them and be conscious about where and how we spend our attention. Attention once spent on something can't be gained back. Attention is also the currency which allows us to do what is most important and accomplish everything that we hold dear and close to ourselves. This is also the currency that we can't make more of. There is a limited amount that we get every day and we need to make the most of what we get.

Attention traps:

There are many kinds of attention traps that we need to be aware of and avoid. Some of the biggest attention traps are wrapped such that they might seem like exactly what we need to do in order to achieve our goals. We need to be vary of them. These may come in the form of a new product, service or even wrapped in a box as a gift. These could come in the form of some amazingly crafted stories shot into movies or in the form of advertisements.

If we still don't believe the kind of power these folks could wield on our lives, I suggest that we go on a technology diet for just a week. Not by going into a place where we don't have access to technology by design, but we need to exercise this diet by our very own self-discipline and we will immediately know the power of these habits that have been induced in us.

Our physiology is programmed to act in a way that is consistent with how it has survived in the past thousands of years. We will do more of anything that will release neuro-chemicals in our brains that are pleasure inducing. We will consistently avoid doing anything that produces neurochemicals that will cause us to feel pain.

People who create products where our attention is their currency are willing to and do exploit these physiological aspects of our attention. They will use every means available to ensure that we consistently take more actions that is in their interest and not in ours.

Technology Traps:

One of the wonders of the world that we live in is the technology that we have developed. The technology allows us to connect with people from faraway lands whom we would have never been able to connect had the technology not existed (social media). Technology allows us to keep ourselves updated on all the current affairs around the world (NEWS, TV). Technology has been instrumental in us increasing our productivity many times over (productivity tools: personal and enterprise). Technology has also enabled us to travel to far off places at a mind-boggling speed (air travel, virtual travel). Technology has also enabled us to access almost anything from anywhere, with almost negligible friction (mobile devices).

And therein lies the problem. As with everything, there are two sides to everything. While technology has provided us all of this, it has also taken away a lot of things. Technology has taken away our ability to connect in person. If we need any proof of this, we can look around us. People are busier with their phones connecting to faraway friends (mostly strangers) and neglect people around them. We have more friends on social media than in our real lives. This is problematic on two different levels. On one side, we live in an illusion of having lots of friends, while having none. This also means that we don't put in the effort that we need to exert in order to make deep friends.

We spend more time on Facebook than with our family. At times, we spend more time on NetFlix and Amazon Prime and Hulu than we spend with our friends and families put together.

The situation has become so bad that some of the industry insiders have become alarmed and have started raising questions among themselves about this race to own our attentions. There are studies which are being run to explore if any of these obsessive behaviours are veering towards addiction.

The early indicators are still not very conclusive, but I can tell from my personal experience that this can be borderline addiction. It becomes more and more difficult to move away from the dopamine (this is a hormone that is produced every time we are expecting a reward from some action. This is exactly the hormone that behaviour designers trigger to keep us coming back or in some cases never leave a product or platform) rush that some of the technology products provide.

It is difficult to move away from a series of stories that end in a way that trigger our need for closure, which in turn means that we will want to go to the next episode to check out what happened and to get closure, only to be lured in to watch the next episode. If this is made simpler (by not need any action from the user) and made automatic, this gets even more difficult.

If you remove the titles of the videos being played one after the other and automatically move to the next episode immediately after the first episode is completed, it can get really difficult for someone to stop and move away. This is the reason why I have personally spent hours together at night watching one episode after the other on Netflix until my body can't take it anymore and dozes off.

The technology providers (including Facebook, Netflix, Amazon, Google and all others) are moving their products towards friction free interaction. What this essentially means is that they want to make using their products or services so easy and automatic that the users can interact with a single click of their mouse and stay connected. Some examples are FaceBook/Instagram's like & share, Amazon's single click checkout, Retweet on Twitter, Next Episode in 5 seconds on Netflix and many more.

Given that this is the case, the question then is what we can do to not act in a way that is beneficial to these players and instead act in a way that is good for us. Here are a few things that I have seen work for me.

1. Do not use any kind of social media, online shopping or Netflix apps on the phone. Our phones are with us all the time and if we use these apps on our phones, we end up using them

all the time as well. If we restrict the use of these tools to the time when we are online on our laptops or desktops, that by itself, limits that time that we can spend on these apps.
2. Stop multitasking while we use these apps. There are so many times when I have caught myself surfing through my Facebook feed or twitter stream when I am eating food or when I am waiting in a queue or when I am walking or when I am waiting for a meeting to begin and even when I am waiting for a traffic signal to turn green from red. Instead, talk to the people around (in front or behind us in the queue), notice and observe people around us and how they behave.
3. Set up an alarm on our phone for the time that we want to spend on any of these platforms and keep the phone across the room, so that we need to get up and move away from the machine to stop the alarm. This very act of getting up and moving away can help us in getting away from the machine.
4. Have technology free time around the home. Especially, technology free eating. It is a well-known fact that families that eat together develop a strong bond with each other. Meetings (with friends or colleagues) can be much better and more productive if done gadget free. Plan your first gadget free meeting and see how that

works for you. Gradually increase this to at least a couple of hours in a day.
5. Turn off all notifications on your phones. Notifications are the hook that keep pulling into the apps and then suck all our attention. Don't give the apps that power to interrupt and grab your attention. The only notification on my phone is when someone calls me. I put my phone on airplane mode when I want to do some serious work.

These are a good place to start. The more comfortable that we become with being in control of our technology use, the more we are the masters of the technology and not the other way around.

Being Curious

One of the things that make us inherently human is our curiosity. Almost every single important invention or discovery can be traced back to someone's curiosity. This is the skill which has had the maximum impact on our and evolution. Every one of us is born curious. We can see this in every child when they are still away from school. The moment we send our kids to school, the curiosity starts declining. The more time that children spend in a school, the less curious they tend to become. At least that seems to be the trend.

When I tried to figure out the reason for this, I find that the entire school experience is designed to make it easier for the teachers to do well and not for the child to do well. Making children (irrespective of their interests and skill levels) sit through the same set of classes, based on their age is to make it easier for the teachers to compare the students. Standardised tests are designed to make it easier for these tests to be administered and then to be evaluated. The standard K-12 is to make it easier for the system to drill in the discipline that these children would need in the corporate workspaces and so that they don't question their bosses when they enter the workforce.

The question then is the following:

How can we help our children (and adults) remain curious?

There are many ways to cultivate our curiosity and one of the best ways that I have found in my experience is by building a habit of looking at things in different perspective.

In his book "Look", author James Gilmore shares a lot of perspectives on active looking. He talks about the different frames of observations:

BINOCULARS LOOKING:

Binoculars looking involves taking a step or two back from the situation and picking a vantage point to better observe the overall scene. Find a place to take in all the action from the best vantage point. We do this so that we can decide what needs to be explored further.

BIFOCALS LOOKING

As they say, nothing is as it appears. Looking with bifocals compares and contrasts different aspects of what's being observed, seeking to uncover various levels and layers of significance. Bifocals looking then alternates between these two different or opposing views.

MAGNIFYING-GLASS LOOKING

Once we have identified an area where we think there are insights to be gained, we use Magnifying-glass looking. This takes a break from other ways of looking to examine one particular feature in much more detail.

MICROSCOPE LOOKING

Once we have looked at a specific feature, it is also important to use microscope looking to slide up and down, left and right, seeking to identify yet more features worth examining. Using this, we look around. We explore the scene by shifting the viewed object itself—to observe even more details at the edges of the scene. Microscope looking involves scrutinising and studying the scene.

ROSE-COLORED-GLASSES LOOKING

Rose-coloured glasses look ahead to improve the scene by uncovering hidden areas. This is when you look at the scene with your own layer added to the scene. This is also when we realise that there is much more than that meets the eye.

BLINDFOLD LOOKING

Having employed the other ways of looking, blindfold looking reflects upon and recalls what was seen (or not seen) and how it was seen (or not). It serves to both summon what has already been noticed and to redirect further looking based on how and why something was missed or mistaken in the scene. This is when you reflect on what you have seen and what was absent that should have been there. This is an area which is often overlooked.

Ask "Why":

Another way to continue to fuel our curiosity is to pay attention to what we look and ask the question – "Why" and pursue the answer to this question, irrespective of what rabbit holes the answer takes us in. Today, we have all the information in the world in our hands. We can find answers to any question we have in a matter of minutes. So, let's use that power to our advantage and continue to explore and flare up our curiosity.

Building Habits

Most of us are creatures of habit. We do most of what we do out of habit and not because we deliberately decided to do it. Habits are like the operating system of our lives. Just like an operating system creates the limits and rules that all other applications on a computer must run, our habits create the limits and rules under which we live out our lives.

Our brain, while being tiny when compared to our body, consumes a disproportionate amount of energy created by our body. So, in order to conserve energy, the brain and our body create routines that become automatic and hence doesn't require active use of our brain thereby reducing the pressure on our body to create a large amount of energy for the brain to consume.

This gives us the possibility to create new routines or habits that we want to introduce. When we look at the computer analogy, our ability to create new habits is like getting access to the operating system and the ability to continually improve it as new applications are being developed all around.

Building a new habit:

It is easier to build a new habit by a process called habit stacking. You take a current habit and add the new habit you want to create to this current habit making the combination your new habit. The old habit will kick in at the stimuli as always and this old habit will then work as the stimuli for the new habit that we want to develop.

For example, we want to build a habit to go for brisk walks every day. Let's assume that you drive to your office and park your car in the parking lot. So, you can start stacking the habit of taking brisk walks to either when you park the car in the morning or just before you take the car out of the parking to leave for home or immediately after you reach your home. All three options can work really well.

The simple way to refer to this is as:

Before/After I do <<Action that you already perform>>, I will do <<The habit that you are trying to build>>.

Replacing an existing habit:

When it comes to habit, creating a new habit is the easiest. The next easiest is replacing existing habits by new habits. In order for us to do this, we need to find out what triggers a habit that we want to replace. For example, if you want to change your habit of watching passive television to developing the habit to read books.

In this case, we need to identify the trigger that leads us to watch television. It could be finishing dinner or sitting on your sofa in your living room or even watching the news in the evening. It could even be feeling stressed or having an argument with your spouse. As you can see the trigger could be an action, an environment or a feeling.

The easiest way to identify the trigger is to notice what is it that you do just before you start watching television. That is most likely the trigger for your current habit. Once you have identified the trigger, you need to then program the new habit that you want to replace this old habit with.

So, assuming that you watch passive television everytime after you finish your dinner. Then you can decide you will start reading a book immediately after you finish your dinner. You might even want to make it easier to read a book after dinner by changing your environment by having a book that you want to read on your dinner table. This will increase your chances of replacing the habit of watching passive television to reading books.

You need to continue to do this every day for a period of time in order for this habit to completely get ingrained.

You can give yourself a much better chance of succeeding at replacing a habit with a newer habit if you could do the following:

- Identify the trigger of your existing habit (emotional, environmental or an action).
- Decide what you want to replace the existing habit with
- Make it extremely easy to do the new action (habit)
- Make it extremely difficult to do the old action (habit)
- Continue to do this until the new habit is totally ingrained.

Dropping a Habit:

Dropping a habit could be extremely easy or extremely tough depending on your personality and the habit that you are trying to drop and the amount of control you have over your environment.

The process to drop a habit starts with identifying the trigger. The best way to drop the habit is then to eliminate this trigger from your environment.

For example, you want to stop watching passive television and don't want to replace it with any new habit.

- The easiest and the fastest way for you to do that is to remove the television from your home. No television, no watching television.
- IF you don't want to go to that extreme, ask your roommate or spouse to hide the remote control from you and not to tell you its location, no matter what.
- The next best way to drop this habit is to create a mechanism so that every minute that you watch passive television, your spouse or partner gets "x" amount of dollars to spend on whatever they want or gets donated to a charity or organization that you hate.

You need to understand that we never live in a vacuum. So, once you successfully drop a habit, something will eventually take its place.

So, my recommendation is to be intentional about what you want to replace the old habit with. Replacing an existing habit with a different habit is always better & easier to accomplish than just dropping a habit.

Storytelling:

We have been a race of story-tellers. We made and told stories even when there was no language – through cave paintings. If we can tell a lie, we can tell stories. This skill is inherent and dormant in each one of us. The question is what can we do to bring out this dormant skill and master it such that we can benefit from it.

Also, each story conveys a message. A story with no message is of no use to anyone. So, before we even start thinking about stories, we need to first decide what is it that we want to convey through the story. Do we want to share our experience ((auto)biographies), wisdom (religious texts), hope (fairy tales, some poetry), knowledge (this book), or to entertain (almost all fiction)?

Depending on what we want to convey, we need to choose the form of the story and then follow the structure of that form.

There are two kinds of stories in my experience. One's that are structured – have a clear beginning, a middle and a definite end. Then there are those which neither have a beginning nor do they have an end. They might start abruptly and end abruptly (and are a part of a larger never-ending story, just like life is never ending).

Another facet of the art of storytelling is to know the audience for the story and what their lives look like. The form and structure of a story for children would be very different from a story that we want to tell to build a certain culture in our organization.

The characters in the stories we tell need to be relatable to the audience to whom the story is being told to.

For example, if you want to encourage your customer support employees to go over and beyond their job descriptions to help your customers, you craft a story where the central character or the hero is a customer support employee, so they can relate to the hero. You create a story about how a customer support employee once dry-cleaned, ironed and delivered a dress personally to a customer, who needed that dress for his wedding. All of this on his own time and at his own expense and thereafter was celebrated by his manager and his manager's manager for this effort.

Instead of creating policies, this one story clearly communicates both to the employees and their managers what they are expected to do.

How to write a story:

1. Relatable characters

2. Known situations
3. Conflicts
4. Emotions
5. Resolution

The first step in telling a good story is to build relatable characters. Characters who have some strengths but also weaknesses. Characters with some flaws. Memorable characters are the first thing that stands out in stories. Each one of us has our own unique and personal mannerisms that we are unconscious about. So, build in these mannerisms that stand out for your character.

Once we have all the characters developed, we need to weave them into a situation. A situation that seems to be too familiar. It could be a situation at work or at home or in a café or someplace else. The situations need to compel the characters to walk into a situation and come face-to-face with the conflict that needs resolution.

How a character resolves the conflict is what gives the strength to the character. The more difficult the conflict, the stronger will the character come out once the same has been resolved. Let the character delve deeper in the conflict. Allow the character to express his/her internal conflict. This makes the characters even more relatable. Allow the character's strengths and flaws to shine.

Every story needs to be emotional. As story tellers we need to already know what kind of emotions we want our audience to feel. That should define what our protagonist feels. That should define how we build the conflict up. That should define how we resolve the conflict.

In resolving the conflict, make the protagonist take a leap of faith or express his strength of personality in the way (s)he resolves the conflict. The resolution should make sense. Just because it is a story doesn't mean that we can resolve a conflict in any which way we deem fit. A good resolution of the conflict will leave the protagonist coming out ahead and at the same time a part of him/her is left behind. Also, the emotion that you want your audience to feel at the resolution will also determine how the conflict is resolved. If you want them to feel inspired, make the protagonist do something that is inspirational. If you want them to feel sad, make the protagonist lose something valuable in the process of resolving the conflict. If you want them to feel content, make the resolution such that the protagonist feels content.

The more difficult the resolution of the conflict, the stronger the protagonist comes out to be.

Developing a story and telling a story are two different crafts. With the above steps, we can develop an interesting story. However, in order to be able to tell it (by words, pictures, sound or video) we need different skills. The most common way to tell these stories is either by using a written medium or by telling the story in-person. When we literally tell a story, we need to understand the nuances of storytelling, like when to pause, how to modulate our tone, when to go faster and when to stop.

When done well, stories can inspire people to take action.

As with everything else, we get better with practice. IF we are leaders and want to use stories to inspire action, we need to practice the stories we want to tell multiple times and tell them again and again, at every opportunity that we get. This will not only make us better but will also reinforce the messaging that we are trying to share with our teams.

The ability to tell good stories is a skill that will allow us to influence and persuade people all around us. There is a reason why I did not include this in the section of persuasive skills. The reason is that good storytelling goes well beyond the ability to persuade. It can inspire, entertain and get people to act or feel a certain way that is much more than just persuasion.

In Conclusion:

We are moving towards a world dominated by smart machines and intelligent algorithms, at an unprecedented pace. We will be eliminating a whole lot of jobs hoping to create a whole lot of new jobs. Whether these jobs will be forthcoming or not is anyone guess. What we can do though is to be prepared for the kinds of work that might get created.

In a world of smart machines and intelligent algorithms, we only have our inherently human capabilities to depend on. Our ability adopt different mindsets based on the need, our ability to adapt to any situation and remain truly human and our ability to stay in control of our attention will be called upon every single day of our existence.

Some may argue that the future that we are talking about where machines and algorithms will take up a whole lot of jobs is still a far distance from now, I believe that it is in our interest that we start getting ready for this future as we speak now.

Whether you are 40 years of age or 14, these mindsets and skillsets that I have shared in this book will help you do well in your life - today, tomorrow and in the future that we are envisaging. So, let's roll our sleeves and get to work!!!!

About the Author:

Mukesh Gupta is an entrepreneur at heart and employee by choice. He considers himself to be a friend, philosopher and a guide for people close to him.

He regularly blogs at www.rmukeshgupta.com and hosts a popular podcast – Pushing Beyond the Obvious, where he holds conversations with practicing entrepreneurs and thought leaders on various topics including Sales, Marketing, Innovation, Leadership, Entrepreneurship and Strategy.

He is also the author of the world's first business poem "Your Startup Mentor".

He lives in Bangalore with his wife (Ichchha) and son (Yuvan)

You can reach him at mgr@rmukeshgupta.com.

Acknowledgements:

There are countless number of people that I need to thank. My wife and son for allowing me to spend time that was rightfully theirs to work on this book.

All my colleagues and friends at work, who have shared their views and debated with me on the topics that I have covered in this book.

All the authors whose works I have referred to in the book, without whose foundational works, this work of mine would not have been possible.

Thanks to the editor of the book - Aishwarya Prakash, who painstakingly read through the book multiple times to ensure that the book reads well and does not have any grammatical errors.

Further Resources:

I would highly recommend reading the following books:

1. Mindset – Carol Dweck
2. Influence – Robert Cialdini
3. Anti Fragile – Nassim Nicholas Taleb
4. Thinking Fast and Slow – Daniel Kahnemann & Amos Taversky
5. Predictably Irrational – Dan Ariely
6. Look – James Gilmore
7. The Power of Habit – Charles Duhigg
8. How to Fail at Almost Everything and still win big – Scott Adams
9. Triggers – Marshall Goldsmith
10. Mastery – Robert Greene
11. Nudge – Richard Thaler

Also, if you want an exhaustive list of books and blogs that you can read, list of people to follow and a list of courses to take, send an email to mgr@rmukeshgupta.com with "Thrive Resources" in the subject line. You will get an email with a list and links to further resources, books, blogs, people and courses.

All rights reserved.
Copyrights @Mukesh Gupta, 2018.

www.ingramcontent.com/pod-product-compliance
Lightning Source LLC
Chambersburg PA
CBHW031627210526
45464CB00004B/1787